Baby Names For Girls That Really Rock (2014)

Louise Nolan

Copyright 2014.

All rights reserved. No part of this book may be reproduced or transmitted in any form or by any means, electronic or mechanical, including photocopying, recording or by any information storage and retrieval system without written permission from the author.

Paperback and electronic versions published by:
Magnificent Milestones, Inc.

ISBN: 9781933819730

Disclaimer:

(1) This book was written as a guide; it does not claim to be the definitive word on baby names. Accordingly, the author and publisher do not accept any liability or responsibility for any loss or damage that have been caused, or allegedly caused, through the use of information in this book.

(2) To our knowledge, all of the information in this book is correct (and current) at the time of publication. However, trends can (and do) change on a daily basis, which will affect the popularity of any given name.

Table of Contents

Chapter 1: Introduction	4
Chapter 2: The Most Popular Baby Names for Girls (2012)	9
Chapter 3: A Blast from the Past - Top Names from the Past Decades	14
Chapter 4. Christian & Biblical Names	20
Chapter 5. Names from Literature & Mythology	23
Chapter 6. Names from Popular Culture / the Entertainment Industry	27
Chapter 7: Named after First Ladies & Daughters	33
Chapter 8. Names from Disney	35
Chapter 9. Names that are Ideals or Concepts	38
Chapter 10. Names from Nature	40
Chapter 11: Last Names as First Names	44
Chapter 12: Named After Famous Places	46
Chapter 13: One Syllable Names	48
Chapter 14: Lengthy (Four Syllable) Names	51
Chapter 15: Unisex / Gender Neutral Names	54
Chapter 16: Popular African-American Names	58
Chapter 17: Popular Hispanic Names	61
Chapter 18: Popular Asian Names	64
Chapter 19. Top 10 Names for Girls in Other Countries	67
Chapter 20: Names with Similar Meanings	69
Chapter 21. Names that Sound Alike	72
Appendix: An Alphabetical List of Names for Girls	75

Chapter 1. Introduction: The Challenges of Choosing the Perfect Name

Few things are more exciting - or complex - than choosing a child's name. The stakes are incredibly high: this beautiful little girl, who has no say in the matter, must live with *your* decision for the rest of her life. Even worse, you must make that decision before you know your daughter's personality and temperament, which determines whether or not the name you have chosen will truly "fit" her.

Years ago, when I perused various books of baby names, I was intrigued by the authors' arbitrary "rules" for first, middle, and last names. Yet, in reality, the beauty of a name is subjective - and what one person considers an excellent choice, another person may not. Thus, I offer only one hard and fast rule in this book: the only opinions that matter are those of the *parents* who will love and raise the baby girl they are naming. Other people may agree or disagree with your choice, but they don't have to live with it - and their input should be considered accordingly.

That being said, there are several factors to consider when choosing a name:

1. **Tradition / Femininity.** Do you want a feminine name or something that is gender neutral? Likewise, do you favor traditional girls' names or something modern or unisex? The difference:

Felicia, Savannah, Evangelina	vs.	Blake, Brett, Flynn
Margaret, Elizabeth, Katherine	vs.	Quinn, Rain, Tai

2. **The family's last name**. Ideally, the child's first, middle, and last names should have a pleasant flow. Ironically, what is "pleasing" to one family may seem harsh and abrupt to another.

For many parents, length and alliteration are also critical. Do you want your child to have a short name that is easy to write and spell - or do you believe that the beauty and flow of a longer name are worth the trade-off?

Patricia Paulina Post	vs.	Jane Lee Post
Millicent Marianna Miles	vs.	Joy Sloan Miles

3. **The uniqueness of the name**. Most parents follow trends, rather than start them. As a result, there are usually five or six students with the same name in every classroom, simply because it was popular the year they were born. In contrast, there will inevitably be one or two students in the same school who have unique names that no one has heard before.

Which of these scenarios do you prefer? Do you want your child to have a popular name that is easy to spell and pronounce, but not particularly creative? Or, do you favor distinctive names that will garner your child (possibly unwanted) attention? The difference:

Sophia Ella White	vs.	Moonbeam Destiny White
Emily Ann Stanton	vs.	Rebel Legend Stanton

Thankfully, there are thousands of names that fall between these two extremes that you can choose, depending upon your personal and familial preferences. When you consider your options, bear in mind: you are making this decision on behalf of a child whose personality may be very different from your own. Are you willing to take a risk - or would you prefer to play it safe?

4. **The longevity of the name**. That cute baby in your arms will eventually become a successful adult with dreams and aspirations of her own. Will the name you choose last a lifetime? In making this decision, consider the following questions - and whether the answers make a difference to you:

a. If given the choice between a physician named Sonia or Buffy, which would you choose?

b. Likewise, can you imagine a district attorney - or circuit court judge - named Bliss or Genesis?

The choice you make will affect how your child is perceived for her *entire life*. What seems "cute" now may not be nearly as desirable on a professional resume.

5. **Consider the initials** your child will have if you choose a particular name. If possible, avoid embarrassing combinations, such as IOU, LOL, PIG, FAG, and WTF. Many times, you can avoid bad combinations by choosing an alternative middle name.

6. If you choose a long or formal name, **consider the nickname** the child is likely to inherit. Some names, such as Katherine and Elizabeth, have multiple options, while others have only one. Even worse, once your child enrolls in school, you are unlikely to control whether or not an undesirable nickname "sticks." Bottom line: if you don't want your kids called Trish or Ginny, don't name them Patricia or Virginia.

7. **Consider the spelling and pronunciation** of the name, which can be a source of confusion and frustration for many children. If you name your child Epiphany or Xaviera, there is an excellent chance that she will spend her entire lifetime explaining to people how to spell and pronounce it. This isn't "bad," per se, but it may be annoying for your child.

8. **Consider the meaning of the name**, if that is important to you. Unfortunately, some popular names have truly awful meanings:

Cameron means "crooked nose"
Kennedy means "ugly head"

Granted, most people do not know - or care about - the meaning of a given name. They simply take it at face value. But if the translation of a name (and the underlying connotation) bothers you, an alternative choice may be best.

9. **Pressures from relatives to choose a "family" name**. There is nothing inherently right or wrong with naming children after beloved relatives. In many cases, it is a lovely way to honor and preserve the memory of someone important to your family. Nevertheless, problems arise when:

a. the name is question is not particularly pleasing
b. the relatives pushing it will not take no for an answer

In these cases, middle names can be an excellent solution. In my experience, a child's middle name is usually chosen for one of three reasons:

a. it is a short, pleasant, and generic "placeholder" between the first and last names:

Examples: Stephanie Ann Miller
                Alexander Lee Ruggerio

b. it is the "second choice" name that was vetoed at the last moment:

Examples: Millicent Marianna Miller
Alexandra Augusta Ruggerio

c. it is the name of a beloved relative that the parents did not want to use as the first name:

Examples: Jennifer Mildred Miller
Jada Esther Ruggerio

Rather than argue with your sister, mother and spouse about a particular choice, using it as a middle name can be a great solution.

10. **Following - or avoiding - trends**. In recent years, there have been several trends in baby names that have influenced parents' choices, including:

- unisex (gender neutral) names
- last names as first names
- naming children after famous places
- creating unique names by adding/deleting letters and changing consonants or vowels
- using names from different cultures or eras
- naming children after celebrities, fictional characters, or historical figures

As a result, baby names are more varied and exotic than ever before. Nevertheless, some parents have resisted these trends in favor of classic and traditional names that will stand the test of time. This book, which presents more than 3,000 names for girls, offers extraordinary choices for *both* groups of parents- and for those who are still sitting on the fence. Use the lists as a starting point - and see what works best for you and your family. Experiment with different names that capture the sound and feel that you desire. Choose the name that perfectly reflects the baby girl you are carrying - and your hopes and dreams for her future.

How to Use this Book

By design, this book is arranged in a logical way:

1. the chapters are clearly labeled to guide your search

2. the names are presented in alphabetical order (unless noted otherwise)

3. the meaning of each name is clearly presented, although some names have multiple meanings, depending upon the original language and interpretation. Due to these variations, we encourage you to conduct additional research into the history and derivation of the names that you choose, both to learn more about them and to explore alternative spellings. By doing so, you can confirm that the name truly feels right and has no negative or unusual connotations.

4. in recent years, parents have expressed a preference for unisex, or gender neutral names that they can use for their babies, regardless of their sex. To honor this request - and to showcase the dozens of names that can be used for both boys and girls, this book presents an entire chapter of unisex names for you to consider.

5. finally, for readers who prefer a direct approach - or simply get tired or overwhelmed by the "themes" we have used, the final chapter of the book presents an alphabetical list of more than 3,000 names for baby girls.

Why 3,000, rather than the 100,000 presented in other books? Because we have streamlined the approach by focusing on the names that you are most likely to use, rather than including odd and esoteric choices from 200 years ago that no one can spell or pronounce. We have also avoided the temptation to turn Katherine into 20 different names, simply by making a few spelling changes.

And, that, ultimately, is the final topic of this chapter: the emerging trend of creating unique and customized names by varying the spelling of a classic name. In most cases, **that** is how most baby name books manage to present 50,000 choices - they include every possible alternative way to spell every name they present. On one hand, that is valid, because many parents like the idea of a unique name. On the other hand, it is somewhat misleading - is the name Caryn really all that different from Karen? And do you really *want* to change the spelling of a classic name - knowing that your child will have to explain, correct, and re-spell it for the dozens of teachers, employers, and business contacts who get it wrong?

How to Create a Unique Baby Name

If the answer is yes, here is a quick summary of how to create a customized name.

1. **Change a consonant:**

C to K: Catherine/Katherine, Crystal/Krystal, Christine/Kristine
C to CH: Cris/Chris, Ciara/Chiara
C to S: Cheryl/Sheryl, Cynthia/Synthia
F to Ph: Filippa/Phillippa, Felicia/Phylicia
G to J: Gillian/Jillian
X to J: Xaviera/Javiera
Z to S: Inez/Ines
H to S: Janesha/Janessa

2. **Change a vowel**:

A to E: Megan/Meagan
A to Y Megan/Megyn
CE to SS: Jocelyn/Josslyn
CI to SH: Lacrecia/Lacresha, Marcia/Marsha
E to Y: Karen/ Karyn, Hailee/Hailey
E to O: Conner/Connor, Ellery/Ellory
E to EI: Andre/Andrei, Keegan/Keigan
EO to E: Geoffrey/Jeffrey
I to Y: Nanci/ Nancy, Brandi/Brandy, Katherine/Kathryn
I to E: Austin/Austen
IE to Y: Debbie/Debby
O to EAU: Bo/Beau
U to EW: Drew/Dru
U to W: Laurence/Lawrence

3. **Add (or subtract) a letter or phrase:**

Add an O: Alphonso/Alphonse
Add an S: Apollo/Apollos
Add an E: Clancy/Clancey, Emil/Emile, Axl/Axel
Add an L: Alan/Allen, Chancellor/Chancelor
Add a "son:" Anders/Anderson
Add a "ton:" Fuller/Fullerton, Jack/Jackson
Add a "de:" Wayne/Dewayne

Add a "mac:" Kenzie/Mackenzie
Add a "lyn:" Brooke/Brooklyn, Joss/Josslyn

4. **Combine two names into one:**

Ashlyn: (American): a combination of Ashley and Lynn
Deandra: (American): a combination of Dee and Andrea
Deangelo: (Italian): a combination of De and Angelo
Kaylin: (American): a combination of Kay and Lynn

5. **Use non-traditional words as names**, such as places, surnames, and personal ideals (such as honor, heaven, and bliss). The chapters in this book will provide the inspiration you need to find distinctive and creative names from unusual and unlikely places. For more traditional parents, we have also included quality choices from history, literature, and the Bible. Use the lists as guidance and inspiration for your search - and choose the name for your baby that truly works best for you.

Chapter 2. The Most Popular Names for Girls

For many prospective parents, this chapter is a logical place to start - with the most popular names for girls in the United States. Ironically, readers like this chapter for two very different reasons: some love the idea of giving their child a popular and trendy name, while others hate the concept - and immediately dismiss all top names from consideration.

Regardless of your own inclination, it's fun to explore the current trends in names on a national basis, if only to know what other parents consider trendy and desirable. As you read and consider each name, you can use this information to add (or subtract) various possibilities from your list.

Finally, a word about "popular" names in a nation as large and diverse as the United States: different names are popular in different regions, depending upon the cultural, spiritual and socioeconomic backgrounds of their residents. In an area with many Asian families, for example, names such as Ling and Ming will be more popular than those in other communities. Likewise, in regions that are predominantly Christian, Biblical names will be more popular than those in communities that are spiritually diverse.

On a practical basis, this information may not affect you (or the choices that you make). But it *does* explain why the variation among children's names is so broad in different parts of the country. In some cities, there will be five Emmas in every classroom, but no one named Ling or Carmella. In other places, there will be several Javieras, but no one named Cynthia or Kristen. Ultimately, the names in this chapter are the most popular in the US *on average*, which may (or may not) reflect the demographics in your own community.

Finally, a quick word about the source of this data, which is the U.S. Social Security Administration (SSA). Every child in the U.S. must have a Social Security number in order to be claimed on his/her parents' federal income tax forms (and to qualify for various benefit programs). Every year, the Social Security Administration records the popularity of names based on these applications and releases that information to the public. The SSA does not, however, break the data down by race or ethnicity - as a result, the rankings are averaged over all U.S. citizens who applied for a Social Security number in their child's name that year.

The names in this chapter are the most popular choices for baby girls who were born in the U.S. in 2012, which is the last year for which data is available. We have presented them in order of popularity, from 1 to 100.

1. Sophia: (Greek & Biblical): wisdom

2. Emma: (English, Danish & German): whole, complete, universal

3. Isabella: (Hebrew): devoted to God; (Spanish): God is bountiful; (Biblical): consecrated to God

4. Olivia: (Spanish & Italian): olive; (Biblical): peace of the olive tree

5. Ava: (Latin America): like a bird

6. Emily: (Latin America): admiring

7. Abigail: (Hebrew): father rejoiced; (Biblical): source of joy

8. Mia: (Italian): my; (Biblical): mine

9. Madison: (English): son of Matthew

10. Elizabeth: (English): my God is bountiful; (Hebrew & Biblical): consecrated to God

11. Chloe: (Greek): verdant, blooming

12. **Ella:** (English); beautiful fairy; (Spanish): she

13. **Avery:** (English): counselor, sage, wise

14. **Addison:** (English): son of Adam

15. **Aubrey**: (English): one who rules with elf-wisdom

16. **Lily/Lilly:** (Hebrew, English & Latin America): lily, blossoming flower

17. **Natalie:** (French): to be born at Christmas; (Slovakian): to be born

18. **Sofia:** (Greek & Biblical): wisdom

19. **Charlotte:** (French): feminine

20. **Zoey:** (Greek): life, alive

21. **Grace/Gracie:** (Latin America): grace of God; (American): land of grace

22. **Hannah:** (English & Hebrew): favor, grace; (Biblical): grace of God

23. **Amelia:** (English & Latin America): industrious, striving

24. **Harper:** (English): musician, harp player

25. **Lillian**: (Latin): resembling the lily

26. **Samantha:** (Hebrew & Biblical): listener of God

27. **Evelyn:** (Celtic): light; (English & Hebrew): life, hazelnut

28. **Victoria:** (Latin America): winner

29. **Brooklyn:** (English): water, stream

30. **Zoe:** (Greek): life, alive

31. **Layla:** (Indian): born at night; (Arabian): dark beauty

32. **Hailey:** (English): hero, field of hay

33. **Leah:** (Hebrew): weary

34. **Kaylee:** (American): pure

35. **Anna:** (Hebrew): favor or grace; (Native American): mother; (Israel): gracious

36. **Aaliyah:** (Arabic): an ascender; (Muslim): exalted; (American): immigrant to a new home

37. **Gabriella:** (Israel & Hebrew): God gives strength; (Italian): woman of God

38. **Allison:** (English): noble, truthful, strong character

39. **Nevaeh:** (American): gift from God, heaven spelled backwards

40. **Alexis**: (English): helper, defender; (Biblical): protector of mankind

41. **Audrey**: (English): noble strength

42. **Savannah:** (Spanish): open plain, field

43. **Sarah:** (Hebrew, Spanish & Biblical): princess

44. **Alyssa:** (Greek): logical

45. **Claire:** (English): clear; (French): bright

46. **Taylor:** (English & French): a tailor

47. **Riley**: (English): from the rye clearing; (Irish): a small stream

48. **Camilla**: (Italian): a noble virgin, a ceremonial attendant

49. **Arianna**: (Greek & Italian): holy

50. **Ashley:** (English & Biblical): lives in the ash tree

51. **Brianna:** (Irish): strong; (Celtic & English): she ascends

52. **Sophie:** (Greek & Biblical): wisdom

53. **Peyton:** (English): village

54. **Bella:** (Hebrew): devoted to God; (Spanish & Latin America): beautiful

55. **Khloe:** (Greek): verdant, blooming

56. **Genesis:** (Hebrew): origin, birth; (Israel): beginning

57. **Alexa**: (Greek, English & Latin America): defender of mankind

58. **Serenity**: (Latin & English): peaceful

59. **Kylie:** (Australian): a boomerang

60. **Aubree:** (English): one who rules with elf-wisdom

61. **Scarlett:** (English): red

62. **Stella:** (French, Italian & Greek): star

63. **Maya**: (Indian): an illusion or dream; (Hebrew): woman of the water

64. **Katherine:** (Irish): clear; (English): pure; (Greek): pure, virginal

65. **Julia:** (French): youthful; (Latin America): soft-haired, youthful

66. **Lucy:** (Latin America): bringer of light

67. **Madelyn:** (Greek): high tower

68. **Autumn:** (English & Latin America): the fall season

69. **Makayla**: (English & Irish): like God

70. **Kayla:** (Irish & Greek): pure and beloved

71. **Mackenzie:** (Irish & Scottish): fair, favored one

72. **Lauren:** (French): crowned with laurel

73. **Gianna:** (Italian): diminutive form of Giovanna, which means God is gracious

74. **Ariana**: (Greek & Italian): holy

75. **Faith:** (English): faithful; (Latin America): to trust

76. **Alexandra**: (Greek, English & Latin America): defender of mankind

77. **Melanie:** (Greek): dark-skinned beauty

78. **Sydney**: (French): from Saint Denis

79 **Bailey:** (English): bailiff, steward, public official

80. **Caroline:** (Mexican): beautiful woman; (French & English): song of happiness

81. **Naomi:** (Hebrew & Israel): pleasant

82. **Morgan:** (Celtic): lives by the sea; (Welsh): bright sea

83. **Kennedy**: (Gaelic): a helmeted chief

84. **Ellie**: (English): a diminutive form of Ellen, which means light

85. **Jasmine:** (Persian): a climbing plant; (English): a fragrant flower

86. **Eva:** (Hebrew, Israel, Indian & Spanish): one who gives life

87. **Skylar**: (English): a scholar

88. **Kimberly:** (English): ruler

89. **Violet:** (French): resembling the flower

90. **Molly:** (Israel & English): bitter

91. **Aria:** (Italian): melody

92. **Jocelyn:** (Latin): cheerful, happy

93. **Trinity**: (Latin): the holy three

94. **London**: (English): capital of England; fortress of the moon

95. **Lydia**: (Greek): beautiful maiden

96. **Madeline:** (Greek): high tower

97. **Reagan:** (Celtic): regal; (Irish): son of the small ruler

98. **Piper**: (English): plays the flute

99. **Andrea**: (Greek & Latin): courageous, strong

100. **Annabelle**: (Italian): graceful and beautiful

Chapter 3. The Evolution of Names Since 1900

While reading this book, you may wonder how (and why) names have evolved over time - and why some of your choices sound really strange to your parents and grandparents. In Chapter 2, we listed the most popular names for baby girls in the United States last year. In this chapter, we will take a look back at the same data at ten-year increments, beginning in 1900.

This exercise is fun for several reasons. First, it will allow you to see the types of names that were popular when your parents and grandparents were making the same decision that you are making today (when no one, and I mean, *no one*, named their baby Axel). Second, it reveals the names that are truly timeless - and those that only stayed popular for a few years. Third, it may spark your interest in names that you might otherwise not have considered, either for your daughter's first or middle name. You've just begun your search; before you consider a trendy name, it's worth looking back at some genuine classics, which were inspired by the leaders and celebrities of their time.

All data is from the official records of the U.S. Social Security Administration. For each year, names are presented in the order of popularity, from 1 to 20.

1900

1. **Mary:** (Biblical, English & Slovakian): bitter
2. **Helen:** (Greek): light
3. **Anna/Ana:** (Hebrew): favor or grace; (Native American): mother; (Israel): gracious
4. **Margaret:** (Greek & Latin America): a pearl
5. **Ruth:** (Hebrew & Israel): companion, friend
6. **Elizabeth:** (English): my God is bountiful; (Hebrew & Biblical): consecrated to God
7. **Florence:** (English): flowering; (Latin America): prosperous
8. **Ethyl:** (English): noble
9. **Marie:** (Latin): bitter
10. **Lillian**: (Latin): resembling the lily
11. **Annie:** diminutive form of Anne, which means favor or grace
12. **Edna:** (Celtic): fire; (Hebrew): rejuvenation; (Israel): spirit renewed
13. **Emma:** (English, Danish & German): whole, complete, universal
14. **Alice:** (Spanish): of the nobility
15. **Bessie**: (English): my God is bountiful
16. **Bertha:** (Germany): bright
17. **Grace:** (Latin America): grace of God; (American): land of grace
18. **Rose:** (English, French & Scottish): flower, a rose; (German): horse, fame
19. **Clara:** (French & Catalonia): clear, bright
20. **Mildred:** (English): gentle counselor

1910

1. **Mary:** (Biblical, English & Slovakian): bitter
2. **Helen:** (Greek): light
3. **Margaret:** (Greek & Latin America): a pearl
4. **Dorothy** (Greek): gift of God
5. **Ruth:** (Hebrew & Israel): companion, friend
6. **Anna/Ana:** (Hebrew): favor or grace; (Native American): mother; (Israel): gracious
7. **Elizabeth:** (English): my God is bountiful; (Hebrew & Biblical): consecrated to God
8. **Mildred:** (English): gentle counselor
9. **Marie:** (Latin): bitter
10. **Alice:** (Spanish): of the nobility
11. **Frances**: (Latin America: free
12. **Florence:** (English): flowering; (Latin America): prosperous
13. **Ethyl**: (English): noble

14. **Lillian**: (Latin): resembling the lily
15. **Gladys:** (Welsh): lame
16. **Rose:** (English, French & Scottish): flower, a rose; (German): horse, fame
17. **Evelyn:** (Celtic): light; (English & Hebrew): life, hazelnut
18. **Edna**: (Celtic): fire; (Hebrew): rejuvenation; (Israel): spirit renewed
19. **Annie**: diminutive form of Anne, which means favor or grace
20. **Louise**: (German): famous warrior

1920

1. **Mary:** (Biblical, English & Slovakian): bitter
2. **Dorothy** (Greek): gift of God
3. **Helen:** (Greek): light
4. **Margaret:** (Greek & Latin America): a pearl
5. **Ruth:** (Hebrew & Israel): companion, friend
6. **Mildred:** (English): gentle counselor
7. **Virginia:** (English, Spanish, Italian & Latin America): pure
8. **Elizabeth:** (English): my God is bountiful; (Hebrew & Biblical): consecrated to God
9. **Frances**: (Latin America) free
10. **Anna/Ana:** (Hebrew): favor or grace; (Native American): mother; (Israel): gracious
11. **Betty:** (English): a diminutive form of Elizabeth, which means my God is bountiful, consecrated to God
12. **Evelyn:** (Celtic): light; (English & Hebrew): life, hazelnut
13. **Marie:** (Latin): bitter
14. **Doris:** (Greek): sea
15. **Alice:** (Spanish): of the nobility
16. **Florence:** (English): flowering; (Latin America): prosperous
17. **Irene:** (Greek & Spanish): peaceful
18. **Lillian**: (Latin): resembling the lily
19. **Louise**: (German): famous warrior
20. **Rose:** (English, French & Scottish): flower, a rose; (German): horse, fame

1930

1. **Mary:** (Biblical, English & Slovakian): bitter
2. **Betty:** (English): a diminutive form of Elizabeth, which means my God is bountiful, consecrated to God
3. **Dorothy** (Greek): gift of God
4. **Helen:** (Greek): light
5. **Margaret:** (Greek & Latin America): a pearl
6. **Barbara:** (Latin America): stranger
7. **Patricia:** (Spanish & Latin America): noble
8. **Joan**: (Hebrew): gift from God; (English): God is gracious
9. **Doris:** (Greek): sea
10. **Ruth:** (Hebrew & Israel): companion, friend
11. **Shirley**: (English): bright meadow
12. **Virginia:** (English, Spanish, Italian & Latin America): pure
13. **Dolores:** (Spanish): woman of sorrow
14. **Jean:** (Hebrew): God is gracious
15. **Elizabeth:** (English): my God is bountiful; (Hebrew & Biblical): consecrated to God
16. **Frances**: (Latin America) free
17. **Lois:** (Israel): good; (German): famous warrior
18. **Joyce:** (English & Latin America): cheerful, merry
19. **Evelyn:** (Celtic): light; (English & Hebrew): life, hazelnut
20. **Alice:** (Spanish): of the nobility

1940

1. **Mary:** (Biblical, English & Slovakian): bitter
2. **Barbara:** (Latin America): stranger
3. **Patricia:** (Spanish & Latin America): noble
4. **Judith:** (Hebrew): praised; (Israel): from Judah
5. **Betty:** (English): a diminutive form of Elizabeth, which means my God is bountiful, consecrated to God
6. **Carol:** (French): melody, song
7. **Nancy**: (Hebrew & English): grace
8. **Linda:** (Spanish): pretty; (English): lime tree; (German): snake, lime tree
9. **Shirley**: (English): bright meadow
10. **Sandra:** (Greek): helper of humanity; (English): unheeded prophetess
11. **Margaret:** (Greek & Latin America): a pearl
12. **Dorothy** (Greek): gift of God
13. **Joyce:** (English & Latin America): cheerful, merry
14. **Joan**: (Hebrew): gift from God; (English): God is gracious
15. **Carolyn:** (English): joy, song of happiness
16. **Judy:** (Hebrew): praised; (Israel): from Judah
17. **Sharon:** (Hebrew & Israel): a flat clearing
18. **Helen:** (Greek): light
19. **Janet:** (Hebrew & English): gift from God
20. **Elizabeth:** (English): my God is bountiful; (Hebrew & Biblical): consecrated to God

1950

1. **Linda:** (Spanish): pretty; (English): lime tree; (German): snake, lime tree
2. **Mary:** (Biblical, English & Slovakian): bitter
3. **Patricia:** (Spanish & Latin America): noble
4. **Barbara:** (Latin America): stranger
5. **Susan:** (Hebrew): graceful lily; (Israel): lily
6. **Nancy**: (Hebrew & English): grace
7. **Deborah:** (Hebrew & Israel): honey bee
8. **Sandra:** (Greek): helper of humanity; (English): unheeded prophetess
9. **Carol:** (French): melody, song
10. **Kathleen:** (English, Irish & French): diminutive of Katherine, which means pure
11. **Sharon:** (Hebrew & Israel): a flat clearing
12. **Karen:** (Greek): pure
13. **Donna:** (Italian): lady
14. **Brenda:** (Gaelic): little raven; (Scandinavian): sword
15. **Margaret:** (Greek & Latin America): a pearl
16. **Diane:** (Latin America): hunter
17. **Pamela:** (Greek, English & Indian): honey
18. **Janet:** (Hebrew & English): gift from God
19. **Shirley**: (English): bright meadow
20. **Carolyn:** (English): joy, song of happiness

1960

1. **Mary:** (Biblical, English & Slovakian): bitter
2. **Susan:** (Hebrew): graceful lily; (Israel): lily
3. **Linda:** (Spanish): pretty; (English): lime tree; (German): snake, lime tree
4. **Karen:** (Greek): pure
5. **Donna:** (Italian): lady
6. **Lisa:** (German): devoted to God; (Israel): consecrated to God
7. **Patricia:** (Spanish & Latin America): noble
8. **Debra:** (Hebrew & Israel): honey bee

9. **Cynthia**: (Greek): moon
10. **Deborah:** (Hebrew & Israel): honey bee
11. **Sandra:** (Greek): helper of humanity; (English): unheeded prophetess
12. **Barbara:** (Latin America): stranger
13. **Brenda:** (Gaelic): little raven; (Scandinavian): sword
14. **Pamela:** (Greek, English & Indian): honey
15. **Nancy:** (Hebrew & English): grace
16. **Sharon:** (Hebrew & Israel): a flat clearing
17. **Cheryl:** (English): beloved
18. **Elizabeth:** (English): my God is bountiful; (Hebrew & Biblical): consecrated to God
19. **Teresa/Theresa:** (Finnish): summer, harvester; (Greek): reaper
20. **Lori:** (English): crowned with laurels

1970

1. **Jennifer**: (English & Welsh): fair one; (English & Celtic): white wave
2. **Lisa:** (German): devoted to God; (Israel): consecrated to God
3. **Kimberly:** (English): ruler
4. **Michelle:** (French & Hebrew): like God, close to God
5. **Amy**: (English, French & Latin America): beloved
6. **Angela:** (Spanish, French, Italian & Latin America): angel
7. **Melissa:** (Greek): honey bee
8. **Tammy:** a diminutive form of Tamara, which means spice, palm tree
9. **Mary:** (Biblical, English & Slovakian): bitter
10. **Tracy:** (English): brave
11. **Julie:** (French): youthful; (Latin America): soft-haired, youthful
12. **Karen:** (Greek): pure
13. **Laura:** (English, Spanish & Latin America): crowned with laurel, from the laurel tree
14. **Christine:** (English): follower of Christ
15. **Susan:** (Hebrew): graceful lily; (Israel): lily
16. **Dawn:** (English): aurora; (Greek): sunrise
17. **Stephanie**: (Greek): crowned in victory
18. **Elizabeth:** (English): my God is bountiful; (Hebrew & Biblical): consecrated to God
19. **Heather**: (English): a flowering plant
20. **Kelly**: (Gaelic & Irish): warrior; (Scottish): wood

1980

1. **Jennifer**: (English & Welsh): fair one; (English & Celtic): white wave
2. **Amanda:** (Latin): much loved
3. **Jessica:** (Israel): God is watching; (Hebrew): rich, God beholds
4. **Melissa:** (Greek): honey bee
5. **Sara(h):** (Hebrew, Spanish & Biblical): princess
6. **Heather:** (English): a flowering plant
7. **Nicole:** (French): victory of the people
8. **Amy**: (English, French & Latin America): beloved
9. **Elizabeth:** (English): my God is bountiful; (Hebrew & Biblical): consecrated to God
10. **Michelle:** (French & Hebrew): like God, close to God
11. **Kimberly:** (English): ruler
12. **Angela:** (Spanish, French, Italian & Latin America): angel
13. **Stephanie:** (Greek): crowned in victory
14. **Tiffany:** (Greek): lasting love
15. **Christina:** (English): follower of Christ
16. **Lisa:** (German): devoted to God; (Israel): consecrated to God
17. **Rebecca:** (Biblical): servant of God
18. **Crystal/Krystal:** (English): jewel; (Latin America): a clear brilliant glass

19. **Kelly:** (Gaelic & Irish): warrior; (Scottish): wood
20. **Erin:** (Irish): peace

1990

1. **Jessica:** (Israel): God is watching; (Hebrew): rich, God beholds
2. **Ashley:** (English & Biblical): lives in the ash tree
3. **Brittany:** (English & Celtic): from Britain
4. **Amanda:** (Latin): much loved
5. **Samantha:** (Hebrew & Biblical): listener of God
6. **Sara(h):** (Hebrew, Spanish & Biblical): princess
7. **Stephanie**: (Greek): crowned in victory
8. **Jennifer**: (English & Welsh): fair one; (English & Celtic): white wave
9. **Elizabeth**: (English): my God is bountiful; (Hebrew & Biblical): consecrated to God
10. **Lauren:** (French): crowned with laurel
11. **Megan:** (Irish): soft and gentle; (Greek): strong and mighty
12. **Emily:** (Latin America): admiring
13. **Nicole:** (French): victory of the people
14. **Kayla:** (Irish & Greek): pure and beloved
15. **Amber:** (Arabic): precious jewel, yellow-brown color
16. **Rachel:** (Hebrew): ewe; (Israel): innocent lamb
17. **Courtney:** (English): courteous
18. **Danielle:** (Hebrew): God is my judge
19. **Heather**: (English): a flowering plant
20. **Melissa:** (Greek): honey bee

2000

1. **Emily:** (Latin America): admiring
2. **Hannah:** (English & Hebrew): favor, grace; (Biblical): grace of God
3. **Madison:** (English): son of Matthew
4. **Ashley:** (English & Biblical): lives in the ash tree
5. **Sara(h):** (Hebrew, Spanish & Biblical): princess
6. **Alexis**: (English): helper, defender; (Biblical): protector of mankind
7. **Samantha:** (Hebrew & Biblical): listener of God
8. **Jessica:** (Israel): God is watching; (Hebrew): rich, God beholds
9. **Elizabeth:** (English): my God is bountiful; (Hebrew & Biblical): consecrated to God
10. **Taylor:** (English & French): a tailor
11. **Lauren:** (French): crowned with laurel
12. **Alyssa:** (Greek): logical
13. **Kayla:** (Irish & Greek): pure and beloved
14. **Abigail:** (Hebrew): father rejoiced; (Biblical): source of joy
15. **Brianna:** (Irish): strong; (Celtic & English): she ascends
16. **Olivia:** (Spanish & Italian): olive; (Biblical): peace of the olive tree
17. **Emma:** (English, Danish & German): whole, complete, universal
18. **Megan:** (Irish): soft and gentle; (Greek): strong and mighty
19. **Grace:** (Latin America): grace of God; (American): land of grace
20. **Victoria:** (Latin America): winner

2010

1. **Isabella:** (Hebrew): devoted to God; (Spanish): God is bountiful; (Biblical): consecrated to God
2. **Sophia:** (Greek & Biblical): wisdom
3. **Emma:** (English, Danish & German): whole, complete, universal
4. **Olivia:** (Spanish & Italian): olive; (Biblical): peace of the olive tree
5. **Ava:** (Latin America): like a bird

6. **Emily:** (Latin America): admiring
7. **Abigail**: (Hebrew): father rejoiced; (Biblical): source of joy
8. **Madison:** (English): son of Matthew
9. **Chloe:** (Greek): verdant, blooming
10. **Mia:** (Italian): my; (Biblical): mine
11. **Addison:** (English): son of Adam
12. **Elizabeth:** (English): my God is bountiful; (Hebrew & Biblical): consecrated to God
13. **Ella:** (English); beautiful fairy; (Spanish): she
14. **Natalie:** (French): to be born at Christmas; (Slovakian): to be born
15. **Samantha:** (Hebrew & Biblical): listener of God
16. **Alexis**: (English): helper, defender; (Biblical): protector of mankind
17. **Lily/Lilly:** (Hebrew, English & Latin America): lily, blossoming flower
18. **Grace:** (Latin America): grace of God; (American): land of grace
19. **Hailey:** (English): hero, field of hay
20. **Alyssa:** (Greek): logical

Chapter 4. Christian & Biblical Names for Girls

Across the U.S., Christian and Biblical names continue to be perennial favorites for both boys and girls. Depending upon your preference, you can follow this trend in a traditional or nonconventional way. Some names, such as Anna and Abigail, are extremely popular, while others, such as Bathsheba and Hagar, are relatively rare. Nevertheless, their place in history and religion gives them a strong global appeal.

In this chapter, we present dozens of Christian and Biblical names in alphabetical order. Find the ones that suit your preference - and add them to your list.

Abigail: (Hebrew): father rejoiced; (Biblical): source of joy
Ada: (English): wealthy; (Hebrew): ornament; (German): noble; (African): first daughter

Angela: (Spanish, French, Italian & Latin America): angel
Anna/Ana: (Hebrew): favor or grace; (Native American): mother; (Israel): gracious

Bathsheba: (Hebrew): oath, voluptuous, famous bearer; (Biblical): seventh daughter
Bernice: (French & Greek): one who brings victory

Bethany: (Hebrew & Israel): a life-town near Jerusalem
Beulah: (Hebrew & Israel): married

Candace: (English): pure, glittering white
Carmel: (Hebrew): garden; (Israel): woodland; (Celtic): from the vineyard

Charity: (English): kindness, generous, goodwill
Chloe: (Greek): verdant, blooming

Claudia: (Spanish & Latin America): lame
Cordelia: (English, Welsh & Celtic): of the sea

Deborah: (Hebrew & Israel): honey bee
Diana: (Greek): divine, goddess of the moon and the hunt

Dinah: (Hebrew & Israel): judgment
Drucilla/Drusilla: (Bible): fruitful, dewy-eyed; (Latin America): mighty

Eden: (Hebrew): delight; (Israel): paradise
Edna: (Celtic): fire; (Hebrew): rejuvenation; (Israel): spirit renewed

Elisha: (Hebrew): God is salvation; (Israel): God is gracious
Elizabeth: (English): my God is bountiful; (Hebrew & Biblical): consecrated to God

Esther: (Hebrew & African): star
Eunice: (Greek): happy, victorious

Eva: (Hebrew, Israel, Indian & Spanish): one who gives life
Eve: (Hebrew): to breathe

Faith: (English): faithful; (Latin America): to trust
Grace/Gracie: (Latin America): grace of God; (America): land of grace

Hagar: (Hebrew): forsaken, flight, famous bearer; (Israel): flight
Hannah: (English & Hebrew): favor, grace; (Biblical): grace of God

Honey: (English): sweet
Hope: (English): trust, faith

Jewel: (English & French): precious gem
Joanna: (Hebrew & French): gift from God

Joy: (French, English & Latin America): rejoicing
Judith: (Hebrew): praised; (Israel): from Judah

Julia: (French): youthful; (Latin America): soft-haired, youthful
Leah: (Hebrew): weary

Lia: (Greek): bearer of good news
Lily: (Hebrew, English & Latin America): lily, blossoming flower

Lois: (Israel): good
Lydia: (Greek): maiden

Magdalena: (Hebrew): from the tower; (Spanish): bitter
Mara: (English, Italian, Hebrew & Israel): bitter

Martha: (Israel): lady
Mary: (Biblical, English & Slovakian): bitter

Merry: (English): joyful, mirthful
Miriam: (Hebrew): rebellious; (Israel): strong-willed

Myra: (Greek): fragrant
Naomi: (Hebrew & Israel): pleasant

Neriah: (Israel): light lamp of the Lord
Olive: (Irish): olive; (Latin America): olive branch, peace

Orpah: (Israel): fawn
Paula: (Latin America): small

Phoebe: (Greek): bright, shining one
Priscilla: (Latin America): ancient

Rebecca: (Biblical): servant of God
Rachel: (Hebrew): ewe; (Israel): innocent lamb

Rhoda: (Greek): roses
Rose: (English, French & Scottish): flower, a rose; (German): horse, fame

Ruby: (English & French): a precious jewel, a ruby
Ruth: (Hebrew & Israel): companion, friend

Sapphira: (Hebrew): sapphire; (Israel): beautiful
Sara(h): (Hebrew, Spanish & Biblical): princess

Sela(h): (Israel): pause and reflect
Sharon: (Hebrew & Israel): a flat clearing

Shiloh: (Hebrew): the one to whom it belongs; (Israel): peaceful
Susannah: (Hebrew): graceful lily; (Israel): lily

Tabitha: (Hebrew): beauty, grace; (Israel): a gazelle
Tamara: (Hebrew): palm tree; (Israel): spice

Zina: (English): welcoming
Zillah: (Hebrew): shade

Zipporah: (Hebrew & Israel): bird
Zemira: (Hebrew & Israel): praised

Chapter 5. Names from Literature & Mythology

Many times, when you encounter a baby name that is mature, sophisticated, with a global appeal, it has its roots in literature and mythology. As expected, the popularity of these names has varied over time (and across geographical borders). Nevertheless, names from literature and mythology continue to hold a strong appeal for American parents who are passionate about history and the arts. In this chapter, we present a comprehensive list of names from literature and mythology in alphabetical order. See if your daughter's name is on the list!

Agatha: (Latin): virtuous, good
Aimee: (English, French & Latin America): beloved

Aja: (Indian): goat
Alejandra: (Spanish): defender of mankind

Anat: (Hebrew & Israel): a singer
Annika: (Dutch): gracious

Antoinette: (French): flower
Aphrodite: (Greek): beauty, love goddess

Apollonia: (Greek): strength
Artemis: (Greek): goddess of the moon

Astraea: (Greek): justice
Athena: (Greek): wisdom, goddess of war

Aurora: (Latin): dawn
Ava: (Latin America): like a bird

Avalon: (Latin): island
Beatrice: (Italian): blesses; (French): bringer of joy

Belisama: (Celtic): goddess of rivers and lakes
Branwen: (Welsh): raven

Bronte: (Greek): thunder
Calliope: (Greek): beautiful voice

Camilla: (Italian): a noble virgin, a ceremonial attendant
Candace: (English): pure, glittering white

Cassandra: (Greek): prophet of doom
Cecilia: (Latin): blind

Chloe: (Greek): verdant, blooming
Cleo/Clio: (English): father's glory

Clair: (English): clear; (French): bright
Cleopatra: (Greek): glory to the father; (African American): queen

Cloris: (Greek): goddess of flowers
Colette: (English): victorious people

Constance: (American): strong-willed
Cordelia: (English, Welsh & Celtic): of the sea

Cynthia: (Greek): moon
Dalia: (Hebrew): tree branch

Daphne: (Greek): of the laurel tree
Dekla: (Latvian): a trinity goddess

Demeter: (Greek): lover of the earth
Echo: (Greek): sound returned

Electra: (Greek): bright, the shining one
Elinor: (English): torch

Eudora: (Greek): honored gift
Eunice: (Latin): victory

Faith: (English): faithful; (Latin America): to trust
Felicia: (French & Latin America): happiness

Felicity: (French, English & Latin America): happiness
Flora: (English): flower: (Latin): flowering

Freya: (Norse): lady
Geraldine: (French, English & German): rules by the spear

Gillian: (English): child of the gods; (Irish): young at heart
Guinevere: (Celtic): white lady; (English): white wave

Harriet: (English & German): rules the home
Helen: (Greek): light

Helene: (French): in the light of the sun
Hera: (Greek): goddess of marriage

Hester: (Greek): star
Hestia: (Greek): goddess of the hearth

Ida: (English): hardworking
Ina: (Polynesian): moon goddess

Isadore/Isadora: (Greek): gift from the goddess Isis
Ishtar: (Arabic): mythical goddess of love and fertility

Isis: (Egyptian): most powerful goddess
Janine: (Hebrew): gift from God

Josephina: (Hebrew): God will add
Juliana: (Spanish): soft-haired

Juno: (Roman): mythical queen of the heavens
Justina: (Greek): just

Justine: (English): just, upright; (Latin America): fairness
Kamala: (Hawaiian & Indian): lotus

Kelly: (Gaelic & Irish): warrior; (Scottish): wood
Laurie: (English): crowned with laurels

Leda: (Greek): mother creator
Lilith: (Babylonian): woman of the night

Livia: (English): life
Lorelei: (German): from the rocky cliff

Lucy: (Latin America): bringer of light
Maeve: (Irish): intoxicating, joyous

Maia: (French): May, (Greek): mother
Marian: (French): bitter

Marianne: (French): bitter
Martha: (Israel): lady

Melia: (German): industrious
Melissa: (Greek): honey bee

Minerva: (Latin): wise
Ming: (Chinese): brilliant light

Mirabel: (Spanish): of uncommon beauty
Morgan: (Celtic): lives by the sea; (Welsh): bright sea

Muriel: (Arabian): myth; (Celtic): shining sea
Natasha: (Greek): rebirth

Nyssa: (Greek): the beginning
Octavia: (Latin America): eighth; (Italian): born eighth

Odessa: (Latin America): the odyssey
Olga: (Slovakian): holy

Ophelia: (Greek): useful, wise
Pandora: (Greek): gifted and talented woman

Patience: (English): patient, enduring
Patricia: (Spanish & Latin America): noble

Penelope: (Greek): weaver
Phoebe: (Greek): bright, shining one

Pomona: (Latin): goddess of fruit trees
Portia: (Latin): offering

Quilla: (Incan): goddess of the moon
Raven: (English): to be black, blackbird

Regina: (Italian, Spanish & Latin America): queen
Rhea: (Greek): rivers

Rosemary: (English): bitter rose
Sabrina: (English): legendary princess

Selene: (Greek): of the moon
Sheila: (English & Irish): blind; (Italian): music

Tess: (English): harvester
Thea: (Greek): gift of God

Ursula: (Danish & Scandinavian): female bear
Venus: (Greek): love goddess, little bird

Winifred: (Irish): friend of peace; (Welsh): reconciled, blessed
Yara: (Brazilian): goddess of the river; (Iranian): courage

Zenia: (Greek): hospitable
Zora: (Slavic): sunrise

Zoya: (Greek): life

Chapter 6. Names from Popular Culture & the Entertainment Industry

Every year, parents seek new inspiration for their babies' names from the world of music, movies, sports, and television. As a result, the rise of a popular athlete, singer, or reality star can have a strong - and immediate - impact on a parent's choice of names. In some cases, such as Adele and Audrey, the phenomenon brings new interest to classic names that had fallen out of favor. In other cases, such as Buffy and Miley, the phenomenon brings new names to the forefront that would otherwise not be considered.

My only caveat about names from popular culture is their shelf-life. Sixty years ago, millions of parents named their baby girls after Marilyn Monroe; however, its popularity waned within a few years. Nevertheless, some trends **do** manage to stick. After *Love Story* was released in 1970, millions of parents named their baby girls after the doomed heroine Jennifer ..... and the name continued to remain a top choice for more than 25 years.

When reviewing these names, try to be objective - and determine if you would still like the name if it was *not* associated with a famous person, character, movie, or song. Also consider the popularity of the name - and whether you want your child to be one of the seven girls named Mila in her kindergarten class. In the end, there is no right or wrong answer - simply what feels right to **you**.

Aaliyah/Aliyah: (Arabic): an ascender; (Muslim): exalted; (American): immigrant to a new home
Addison: (English): son of Adam

Adele: (German & French): noble, kind
Alanis: (English): attractive

Alexis: (English): helper, defender; (Biblical): protector of mankind
Alyssa: (Greek): logical

Amber: (Arabic): precious jewel, yellow-brown color
America: (English): ruler of the home

Angelina: (Italian): little angel
Anjelica: (Greek): a diminutive form of Angela, which means angel

Aria: (Italian): melody
Arial: (Hebrew): lioness of God

Arianna: (Greek & Italian): holy
Ashanti: (African): great African woman

Ashley: (English & Biblical): lives in the ash tree
Audrey: (English): noble strength

Audrina: (English): nobility, strength
Avril: (English): born in April

Bailey: (English): bailiff, steward, public official
Bella: (Hebrew): devoted to God; (Spanish & Latin America): beautiful

Bettina: (English): consecrated to God
Beyonce: (American): one who surpasses others

Bijou: (French): as precious as a jewel
Blair: (Irish & Celtic): from the plain, (Gaelic): child of the fields; (Scottish): peat moss

Blythe: (English): happy
Brandy: (English): firebrand

Bree: (Celtic): broth; (Irish): hill, strong one
Bristol: (English): bridge

Brittany: (English & Celtic): from Britain
Bronwyn: (Welsh): dark and pure; (English): white-skinned

Brooke: (English): lives by the stream
Brooklyn: (English): water, stream

Buffy: (American): buffalo, from the plains
Carmen: (English): garden; (Spanish & Latin America): song

Carrie: (American): melody, song
Cameron/Camryn: (Irish & Gaelic): crooked nose

Camilla/Camille: (Italian): a noble virgin, a ceremonial attendant
Campbell: (Scottish): crooked mouth

Callie/Cally: (Greek): beautiful; (English); lark
Carlie/Carly: (American): strong one; (Latin America): little, womanly

Celine: (Latin): of the heavens
Charisma: (Greek): grace

Charlize: (French): manly
Cher: (English): beloved

Chloe: (Greek): verdant, blooming
Clove: (German): spice

Clover: (English): meadow flower
Contessa: (Italian): a countess

Cordelia: (English, Welsh & Celtic): of the sea
Courtney: (English): courteous

Crimson: (English): deep red color
Dana: (English, Danish, Irish & Hebrew): a person from Denmark

Danica: (Slavic): the morning star
Destiny: (English): fate

Dharma: (Indian): ultimate law of all things
Dionne: (Greek): divine queen

Dominique: (French): belonging to God
Drew: (Greek): courageous, strong

Edie: (English): blessed
Effie: (Greek): melodious talk

Elle: (English): torch
Elliott: (Israel): close to God; (English): the Lord is my God

Evangeline: (Greek): like an angel
Faith: (English): faithful; (Latin America): to trust

Fantasia: (Latin): from a fantasy land
Felicity: (French, English & Latin America): happiness

Fiona: (Gaelic): fair, a white-shouldered woman
Florence: (English): flowering; (Latin America): prosperous

Gabrielle: (French): strength of God
Giada: (Italian): jade

Giselle: (French): pledge
Giuliana: (Italian):youthful

Golda/Goldie: (English): resembling the precious metal
Gwyneth: (Welsh): blessed with happiness

Hallie/Halle: (English): hay meadow
Hannah: (English & Hebrew): favor, grace; (Biblical): grace of God

Harlow: (American): impetuous
Harper: (English): musician, harp player

Haven: (English): safe place
Hayden: (English & Welsh): in the meadow or valley

Haylee/Hailey: (English): from the hay meadow, hero
Hazel: (English & Irish): the hazel tree

Hermione: (Greek): earthly
Hillary: (English & Greek): joyous, cheerful

Hoda: (Indian): child of God
Honor: (Spanish & Irish): honor; (Latin America): integrity

Ilsa: (German): abbreviation of Elizabeth, which means God is bountiful
Ireland: (Irish): country of the Irish

Ivanka: (Slavic): God is gracious
Ivy: (English): vine

Jada: (Israel): wise
Jamie: (English): supplanter, representative

Jamielynn: (American): a combination of Jamie and Lynn
January: (American): born in January

Jewel: (English & French): precious gem
Jorja: (English): farmer

Juno: (Roman): mythical queen of the heavens
Katniss: (American): female warrior

Keira: (Celtic): black-haired
Keisha: (African): favorite

Kendall: (English & Celtic): from the bright valley
Kendra: (English): having royal power

Kerri: (Irish): dusky, dark
Kimora: (American): royal

Kristi: (Greek): anointed, follower of Christ
Kyle: (Irish): attractive

Kylie: (Australian): a boomerang
Lacy/Lacey: (Irish): surname; (English): derived from lace

Lake: (American): body of water, from the lake
Layla: (Indian): born at night; (Arabian): dark beauty

Leighton: (English): herb garden, town by the meadow
Liberty: (English): free, independent

Lorelei: (German): from the rocky cliff
Madonna: (Italian): my lady

Malia: (American): calm, peaceful
Mariah: (English): biter

Martina: (Latin America): warlike
Meredith: (Welsh): great ruler, protector of the sea

Michelle: (French & Hebrew): like God, close to God
Miley: (American): virtuous

Miranda: (Latin): worthy of admiration
Mischa: (Russian): like God

Monique: (French): one who provides wise counsel
Monroe: (Gaelic): from the red swamp; (Scottish): from the river; (Irish): near the river roe

Montana: (Latin America): mountainous
Murphy: (Irish): sea warrior

Mya: (American): emerald
Nadia: (Slovakian): hopeful

Neve: (Irish): radiant
Nicole: (French): victory of the people

Nicolette: (French): a form of Nicole, which means victory of the people
Nikita: (Russian): victorious people

Nona: (English): ninth
Octavia: (Latin America): eighth; (Italian): born eighth

Oprah: (Hebrew): resembling a fawn
Quinn: (Celtic): wise; (Irish): fifth, counsel, intelligent

Paris: (Persian): angelic face; (Greek): downfall; (French): the capital city of France
Penelope: (Greek): weaver

Peyton: (English): village
Philippa/Pippa: (English): friend of horses

Phoebe: (Greek): bright, shining one
Piper: (English): plays the flute

Portia: (Latin): offering
Posy: (English): God will increase

Primrose: (English): the first rose, primrose flower
Precious: (American): treasured

Prudence: (English): prudent or cautious
Rachel: (Hebrew): ewe; (Israel): innocent lamb

Rain/Raina: (American): blessings from above; (French & Latin): ruler; (English): lord, wise
Reba: (Hebrew): fourth

Rebel: (American): outlaw
Reese/Reece: (English &Welsh): ardent, fiery, enthusiastic

Remy: (French): oarsman or rower, from Rheims
Rhianna: (English): goddess; (Welsh): nymph

Rhoda: (Greek): roses
Rielle: (Hebrew): a feminine form of Gabriel, which means God is my strength

Riley: (Irish): a small stream
Rory: (Irish): famous brilliance, famous ruler; (Gaelic): red-haired

Rosario: (Filipino & Spanish): rosary
Roseanna: (Greek): graceful rose

Roseanne: (Greek): graceful rose
Rue: (English): bitter, medicinal plant

Rumer: (English): gypsy
Santana: (Spanish): saintly

Sasha: (English): defender of mankind
Scarlett: (English): red

Sela(h): (Israel): pause and reflect
Selena: (Greek): of the moon

Serena: (English): calm, serene
Shakira: (Arabic): grateful

Shanae: (Hebrew): God is gracious
Shania: (Native American): on my way

Shannon/Shannen: (Gaelic): having ancient wisdom
Sherri: (Israel): beloved; (French): dear one

Sheryl: (English): beloved
Shiloh: (Israel): peaceful

Sinead: (Irish): gift from God
Sienna: (Italian): reddish brown in color

Signourney: (English): victorious conquerer
Simone: (French): one who listens well

Solange: (French): religious and dignified
Soledad: (Spanish): solitary

Summer: (English): the summer season
Sunshine: (English): brilliant rays from the sun

Suri: (Todas): pointy nose
Sydney: (French): from Saint Denis

Tameka: (Aramaic): twin
Tanya: (Slovakian): a fairy queen

Taylor: (English & French): a tailor
Temperance: (English): temperate, moderate

Thora: (Scandinavian): thunder
Tiana: (Greek): princess

Tipper: (Irish): water pourer
Topagna: (Native American): from above

Tory/Tori: (American): victorious
Trisha: (English & Latin): noble

Tyra: (Scandinavian): God of battle; (Scottish): land
Uma: (Hindi): mother

Unique: (Latin): only one; (American): unlike others
Venus: (Greek): love goddess, little bird

Vera: (Russian): verity, truth
Vivianne: (English): the lady of the lake

Whitney: (English & African American): white island
Willow: (English): willow tree

Wynonna/Winona: (American): oldest daughter
Xena: (Greek): hospitable

Yasmine/Yasmeen: (Persian): resembling the jasmine flower
Zahara: (Arabic): shining, luminous

Zoe (or Zoey): (Greek): life, alive

Chapter 7. Named After First Ladies & Presidential Daughters

The names of U.S. Presidents and First Ladies are favorites for many prospective parents. This is particularly true in election years, when the country "meets" the candidates' spouses and families for the first time. In this chapter, we will explore the names of First Ladies and children that have stood the test of time; they also provide a fascinating glimpse into the distinguished women who have lived in the White House during the past two centuries.

Abigail: (Hebrew): father rejoiced; (Biblical): source of joy
Amy: (English, French & Latin America): beloved

Anjelica: (Greek): a diminutive form of Angela, which means angel
Anna/Anne: (Hebrew): favor or grace; (Native American): mother; (Israel): gracious

Barbara: (Latin America): stranger
Caroline: (Spanish): beautiful woman; (French & English): song of happiness

Chelsea: (English): seaport
Claudia: (Spanish & Latin America): lame

Dolly: (American): cute child
Edith: (English): joyous, a treasure

Eleanor: (English): torch
Eliza: (French): consecrated to God

Elizabeth: (English): my God is bountiful; (Hebrew & Biblical): consecrated to God
Ellen: (Greek): light

Emily: (Latin America): admiring
Florence: (English): flowering; (Latin America): prosperous

Frances: (Latin America): free
Grace: (Latin America): grace of God; (American): land of grace

Harriet: (English & German): rules the home
Helen: (Greek): light

Hillary: (English & Greek): joyous, cheerful
Ida: (English): hardworking

Jacqueline: (French): to protect
Jane: (Hebrew): gift from God; (English): gracious, merciful

Jenna: (English): small bird
Julia: (French): youthful; (Latin America): soft-haired, youthful

Laura: (English, Spanish & Latin America): crowned with laurel, from the laurel tree
Leticia: (Spanish): joy, gladness

Lou/Louisa: (German): famous warrior
Lucrecia: (Spanish): brings light

Lucy: (Latin America): bringer of light
Malia: (American): calm, peaceful

Mamie: (American): a diminutive form of Margaret, which means pearl
Margaret: (Greek & Latin America): a pearl

Martha: (Israel): lady
Mary: (Biblical, English & Slovakian): bitter

Maureen: (Irish): star of the sea, from the sea of bitterness
Michelle: (French & Hebrew): like God, close to God

Nancy: (Hebrew & English): grace
Priscilla: (Latin): from an ancient family

Rose: (English, French & Scottish): flower, a rose; (German): horse, fame
Rosalind: (Spanish): beautiful one

Sasha: (English): defender of mankind
Sara(h): (Hebrew, Spanish & Biblical): princess

Chapter 8. Names from Disney

In reality, this material could easily be included in Chapter 6, which presents baby names from popular culture and the entertainment industry. But, on a practical basis, Disney has a greater reach - and longer staying power - than most musical, athletic, and movie franchises, which is why we have given it a chapter all its own.

Within a few months of a Disney release, the names of its characters begin to ascend the list of popular baby names. As a result, they bring the same benefits and pitfalls of other trendy names: everyone knows why you chose it..... and they probably chose it, too!

In the past few years, here are the most popular girls' names from Disney movies (in alphabetical order). See if one of them is right for *your* little princess.

Abigail: (Hebrew): father rejoiced; (Biblical): source of joy
Adelaide: (French & German): noble, kind

Adella: (German & French): noble, kind
Alana: (Irish): beautiful, peaceful

Alice: (Spanish): of the nobility
Amelia: (English & Latin America): industrious, striving

Anastasia: (Greek): resurrection
Andrina: (English): courageous, valiant

Anita: (Italian, Hebrew & Latin America): gracious
Ariel: (Hebrew): lioness of God

Arista: (Latin): harvest
Audrey: (English): noble strength

Aurora: (Latin): dawn
Bambi: (Italian): child

Barbie: (Latin America): a diminutive form of Barbara, which means stranger
Belle: (French): beautiful

Bianca: (Italian): white, fair
Bonnie: (English): good; (French): sweet; (Scottish): pretty, charming

Calliope: (Greek): beautiful voice
Carlotta: (Italian): a derivative of Charlotte, which means feminine

Celia: (Italian): heavenly
Charlotte: (French): feminine

Cinderella: (French & English): of the ashes
Clarabelle: (French & Catalonia): clear, bright/(French): beauty

Cleo: (English); father's glory
Colette: (English): victorious people

Daisy: (English); day's eve; (American): daisy flower
Dinah: (Hebrew & Israel): judgment

Donna: (Italian): lady
Dori/Dory: (Greek): gift

Elizabeth: (English): my God is bountiful; (Hebrew & Biblical): consecrated to God
Ellie: (English): a diminutive form of Ellen, which means light

Esmeralda: (Spanish): resembling a prized emerald
Eudora: (Greek): honored gift

Evangeline: (Greek): like an angel
Faline: (Irish): in charge

Fauna: (French): fawn, a young deer
Felicia/Felice/Phylicia: (French & Latin America): happiness

Flora: (English): flower: (Latin): flowering
Frances: (Latin America): free

Genia/Genie: (Greek): well-born
Giselle: (French): pledge

Georgette: (French): farmer
Gypsy: (English): wanderer

Helga: (German): wealthy, blessed
Hera: (Greek): Goddess of marriage

Jane: (Hebrew): gift from God; (English): gracious, merciful
Jasmine: (English): a fragrant flower

Jessica/Jessie: (Israel): God is watching; (Hebrew): rich, God beholds
Kala: (Hawaiian): princess

Kay: (Greek): rejoice; (Scottish & Welsh): fiery
Kirby: (Scandinavian): church village

Laverne: (French): woodland, like the spring
Lilo: (American): generous one

Ling: (Chinese): dainty
Marian: (French): bitter

Marie: (Latin): bitter
Megara: (Greek): wife of Hercules

Melody: (Greek): beautiful song
Minnie: (Irish): bitter; (Hebrew): wished for a child

Morgana: (Welsh & Celtic): dweller of the sea
Mulan: (Chinese): magnolia blossom

Myrtle: (Greek): the tree, victory; (English): the flowering shrub
Nala: (African): successful; (Tanzanian): queen

Olivia: (Spanish & Italian): olive; (Biblical): peace of the olive tree
Penny: (English): duck

Perdita: (English): lost
Rosie: (English, French & Scottish): flower, a rose; (German): horse, fame

Roz: (Polish): rose
Sally/Sallie: (English): princess

Sara(h): (Hebrew, Spanish & Biblical): princess
Seraphina: (Israel): burning fire; (Hebrew): fiery-ringed

Snow: (American): frozen rain
Thalia: (Greek): plentiful, blooming

Tia: (Greek); princess; (Spanish): princess, aunt; (African American): aunt
Tiana: (Greek): princess

Ursula: (Danish & Scandinavian): female bear
Vanessa: (Greek): resembling a butterfly

Violet: (French): resembling the flower
Wendy: (English): white-skinned, literary

Wilhemina: (German): resolute protector
Willow: (English): willow tree

Winifred: (Irish): friend of peace; (Welsh): reconciled, blessed

Chapter 9. Names that are Ideals or Concepts

A fascinating trend is the use of personal ideals - such as Charity and Fidelity - as baby names. These noble concepts are valued in all cultures, which gives the names a global appeal. Additionally, most of them are relatively rare, which increases their cachet. In this chapter, we present a list of concept names for baby girls (in alphabetical order). Perhaps one of them will be right for your little angel.

Angel: (Spanish & Greek): angelic
Bliss: (English): joy, happiness

Cadence: (Latin): rhythmic and melodious
Charity: (English): kindness, generous, goodwill

Chastity: (Latin): pure
Cherish: (English): to be held dear, values

Destiny: (English): fate
Dharma: (Indian): ultimate law of all things

Epiphany: (Greek): manifestation
Ever: (English): strong as a boar

Faith: (English): faithful; (Latin America): to trust
Felicity: (French, English & Latin America): happiness

Fidelity: (Latin): faithful, true
Flair: (English): natural talent

Flame: (American): passionate, fiery
Gay: (English): merry, happy

Grace: (Latin America): grace of God; (American): land of grace
Harmony: (Latin America): a beautiful blending

Haven: (English): safe place
Heaven: (American): from the heavens

Honor: (Spanish & Irish): honor; (Latin America): integrity
Hope: (English): trust, faith

Journey: (American): one who likes to travel
Joy: (French, English & Latin America): rejoicing

Liberty: (English): free, independent
Love: (English): full of affection

Maven: (English): having great knowledge
Mercy: (English): compassion; (French): merciful

Merry: (English): joyful, mirthful
Patience: (English): patient, enduring

Peace: (English): peaceful
Prudence: (English): prudent or cautious

Rebel: (American): outlaw
Salome: (Hebrew): peace and tranquility

Serenity: (Latin & English): peaceful
Unique: (Latin): only one; (American): unlike others

Unity: (American): unity, togetherness
Victory: (Latin): victory

Chapter 10. Names from Nature

People differ greatly in their temperament and ideals. Many times, our only commonality is the planet we inhabit - and the beautiful flowers, oceans, colors, and gemstones that we all enjoy. As a result, names from nature are perennial favorites for girls in all cultures. In this chapter, we present an intriguing collection of girls' names that honor the incomparable beauty of nature.

Names of Flowers, Fruit & Spices

Amaranth: (Greek): an unfading flower
Apple: (American): sweet fruit

Blossom: (English): fresh, flowerlike
Brandy: (English): a woman wielding a sword, an alcoholic drink

Calla: (Greek): resembling a lily, beautiful
Candy: (American): bright, sweet; (Hebrew): famous bearer

Cayenne: (French): hot and spicy
Cherise: (French): cherry, dear one

Cherry: (French): dear one; (American): cherry
Cinnamon: (American): reddish-brown spice

Clover: (English): meadow flower
Coral: (English): a reef formation

Daisy: (English); day's eve; (American): daisy flower
Fern: (English): the fern plant

Flora: (English): flower: (Latin): flowering
Gardenia: (English): a sweet-smelling flower

Ginger: (English): the spice
Heather: (English): a flowering plant

Holly: (French, English & Germany): shrub
Honey: (English): sweet

Iris: (Greek): colorful, rainbow; (Hebrew & English): the flower
Ivy: (English): vine

Jasmine: (Persian): a climbing plant; (English): a fragrant flower
Laurel: (English & French): crowned with laurel, from the laurel tree

Lavender: (English): a purple flowering plant
Leighton: (English): herb garden, town by the meadow

Lilac: (Latin America): bluish purple; (American): a flowering bluish purple shrub
Lily: (Hebrew, English & Latin America): lily, blossoming flower

Lotus: (Greek): the flower
Meadow: (American): beautiful field

Olive: (Irish): olive; (Latin America): olive branch, peace
Peaches: (English): fruit

Petunia: (English): resembling the flower
Poppy: (English & Latin America): the poppy flower

Rose: (English, French & Scottish): flower, a rose; (German): horse, fame
Rosemary: (English): bitter rose

Saffron (English): resembling the yellow flower
Sage: (English & French): wise one; (English): from the spice

Violet: (Italian): violet flower
Willow: (English): willow tree

Zinnia: (English): the flower: (Latin America): beautiful

Colors

Amber: (Arabic): precious jewel, yellow-brown color
Blue: (English): the color blue

Crimson: (English): deep red color
Coral: (English): a reef formation

Cyan: (American): light blue or green
Ebony: (American): dark strength

Fuschia: (Latin): resembling the color
Goldie: (English): resembling the precious metal

Indigo: (Latin America): dark blue
Ivory: (English & Latin America): white, pure

Lavender: (English): a purple flowering plant
Mauve: (American): purplish color

Scarlett: (English): red
Sienna: (Italian): reddish brown in color

Silver: (English): the color silver
Violet: (Italian): violet flower

Names of Gemstones

Amber: (Arabic): precious jewel, yellow-brown color
Amethyst: (Greek): a semi-precious stone **Beryl:** (Greek & English): green jewel

Azura/Azure: (Persian): a blue, semi-precious stone
Cameo: (Italian): sculptured jewel; (English & Latin America): a shadow or carved gem portrait

Crystal/Krystal: (English): jewel; (Latin America): a clear brilliant glass
Diamond: (English): bridge protector: (Greek): unbreakable

Emerald: (English, Spanish & French): a bright green gem
Garnet: (English): gem, armed with a spear; (French): keeper of grain

Gemma: (French & Italian): jewel
Jade: (Spanish): jewel, green gemstone

Jewel: (English & French): precious gem
Onyx: (Greek): the onyx stone

Opal: (English & Indian): precious gem
Pearl: (English): gemstone

Ruby: (English & French): a precious jewel, a ruby
Sapphire: (Greek): the sapphire gem; (Hebrew): sapphire gem, beautiful

Topaz/Topaza: (Mexican): golden gem

Names from Weather, Seasons, Nature & Animals

April: (English): opening buds of spring; (Latin America): opening, fourth month
Aurora: (Latin): dawn

Autumn: (English & Latin America): the fall season
Bay: (Vietnam): born on a Saturday

Brooke: (English): lives by the stream
Bunny: (Greek): a diminutive form of Beatrice, which means blessed, happy

Dawn: (English): aurora; (Greek): sunrise
Dove: (American): bird of peace

Easter: (American): from the holiday or Christian festival
Fauna: (French): fawn, a young deer

Fawn: (French & English): young deer
January: (American): the first month of the year

June: (Dominican Republic): born in June
Lake: (American): body of water, from the lake

Lark: (English): a lark; (American): songbird
Luna: (Latin & Latin America): the moon

Marina: (Greek & Slovakian): from the sea
May: (English): name of month; (Hebrew & Latin America): from Mary

Rain/Raine: (American): blessings from above; (French & Latin): ruler; (English): lord, wise
Rainbow: (English): rainbow

Raven: (English): to be black, blackbird
River: (Latin & French): stream, water

Robin: (English): a small bird
Sailor: (American): sailor

Skye: (English): sky
Snow: (American): frozen rain

Spring: (English): the spring season
Starr: (English & American): star

Stormy: (English): tempest; (American): impetuous nature
Summer: (American): the summer season

Sunshine: (English): brilliant rays from the sun
Una: (Welsh & Celtic): white wave; (Native America): remember; (English): one

Ursula: (Danish & Scandinavian): female bear
Winter: (American): the season

Wren: (Welsh): ruler; (English): small bird

Chapter 11. Last Names as First Names

In the past decade, one of the most popular trends is the use of last names as first names for both boys and girls. This approach offers parents a creative way to honor a cherished surname or to give their child a gender neutral (unisex) moniker that will be easy to remember. Alternatively, these choices also make excellent middle names.

In this chapter, we have included the most popular pairs of last names as first names (in alphabetical order). Use the list to narrow your search - or as inspiration for your own unique choices.

Abbott: (Hebrew): father
Alton: (English): from the old town

Avery: (English): counselor, sage, wise
August: (German): revered

Addison: (English): son of Adam
Anderson: (Scottish): son of Andrew

Bailey: (English): bailiff, steward, public official
Brown: (English): brown color, dark-skinned

Bowen: (Gaelic): small son; (Irish): archer
Blake: (English): pale, fair

Brady: (Irish): a large-breasted woman
Blair: (Irish & Celtic): from the plain, (Gaelic): child of the fields; (Scottish): peat moss

Campbell: (Gaelic): crooked mouth; (French): from the beautiful field
Cullen: (Irish & Gaelic): handsome; (Celtic): cub; (English): city in Germany

Casey: (Celtic & Gaelic): brave; (Irish): observant, alert, brave; (Spanish): honorable
Cameron: (Irish & Gaelic): crooked nose

Drew: (English): courageous, valiant
Davis: (English & Scottish): David's son

Emerson: (English): brave, powerful
Elliott: (Israel): close to God; (English): the Lord is my God

Flynn: (Irish): ruddy complexion
Gannon: (Irish & Gaelic): fair-skinned

Jordan: (Hebrew): to flow down; (Israel): descendant
Jensen: (Scandinavian): God is gracious

Kane: (Welsh): beautiful; (Gaelic): little warrior
Keaton: (English): from the town of hawks

Kendall: (English & Celtic): from the bright valley
Kennedy: (Scottish): ugly head; (Irish & Gaelic): helmeted

London: (English): fortress of the moon
Mackenzie: (Irish & Scottish): fair, favored one

Morgan: (Celtic): lives by the sea; (Welsh): bright sea
Marlowe: (English): from the hill by the lake

Madison: (English): son of Matthew
Monroe: (Gaelic): from the red swamp; (Scottish & Irish): near the river roe

North: (English): from the north
Moore: (French): dark-skinned; (Irish & French): surname

Murphy: (Gaelic): warrior of the sea
Peyton: (English): village

Reagan: (Celtic): regal; (Irish): son of the small ruler
Riley: (Irish): a small stream

Ryan: (Gaelic): little king; (Irish): kindly, young royalty
Rowan: (Irish): red-haired; (English & Gaelic): from the rowan tree

Reese: (Welsh): enthusiastic
Rylan: (English); dweller in the rye field

Quinn: (Celtic): wise; (Irish): fifth, counsel, intelligent
Shea: (Irish): majestic, fairy place

Silver: (English): the color silver
Sawyer: (English): one who works with wood

Taylor: (English & French): a tailor
West: (English): from the west

Winter: (American): the season

Chapter 12. Named After Famous Places

This chapter explores a fascinating trend that has emerged in the past two decades: the use of city, state, and country names for both boys and girls. Some of these choices are fairly common, such as Augusta and Charlotte, while others are esoteric, such as Aspen and Darby. Nevertheless, the trend is real, the names are eclectic, and the variety can't be beat. So, sit back and explore the most popular girls' names (in alphabetical order) that are based on famous places.

Aurora: (Latin): dawn
Augusta: (Latin): venerable, majestic

Afton: (English): from the Afton River
Ada: (English): wealthy; (Hebrew): ornament; (German): noble; (African): first daughter

Asia: (Greek & English): resurrection, rising sun
Arizona: (Native American): from the little spring, from the state of Arizona

Aspen: (English): from the aspen tree
Alexandria: (Greek, English & Latin America): defender of mankind

Brooklyn: (English): water, stream
Bristol: (English): bridge

Catalina: (Spanish): pure
Carolina: (Mexican): beautiful woman; (French & English): song of happiness

Chelsea: (English): seaport
Charlotte: (French): feminine

Cheyenne: (French): dog; (Native American): an Algonquin tribe
China: (Chinese): fine porcelain

Dakota: (Native American): friend, ally
Darby: (Irish & Gaelic): free man; (English): deer park

Eden: (Hebrew): delight; (Israel): paradise
Echo: (Greek): sound returned

Florence: (English): flowering; (Latin America): prosperous
Fallon: (Irish): of a ruling family

Georgia: (Greek & German): farmer
Geneva: (French): juniper berry: (German): of the race of woman

Helena: (Greek): light
Hailey/Hailee/Haley: (English): hero, field of hay

Ireland: (Irish): of a ruling family
India: (English): from India

Jordan: (Hebrew): to flow down; (Israel): descendant
Logan: (Irish): small cove; (Scottish): Finnian's servant; (Gaelic): from the hollow

Kent: (English & Welsh): white; (Celtic): chief
Kenya: (Israel): animal horn

Lincoln: (English): Roman colony at the pool; (Latin America): village
Lane: (English): narrow road, from the long meadow

Madison: (English): son of Matthew
Montana: (Latin America): mountainous

Nazareth: (Hebrew): religion
Nevada: (English): covered in snow

Odessa: (Latin America): the odyssey
Octavia: (Latin America): eighth; (Italian): born eighth

Paris: (Persian): angelic face; (Greek): downfall; (French): the capital city of France
Phoenix: (Greek): rising bird

Regina: (Italian, Spanish & Latin America): queen
Racine: (French): root

Sierra: (Spanish): mountain; (Irish): dark
Savannah: (Spanish): open plain, field

Virginia: (English, Spanish, Italian & Latin America): pure
Vienna: (Latin America): from wine country

Sydney: (English): wide island
Sahara: (Arabian): wilderness

Victoria: (Latin America): winner
Valencia: (Spanish): brave

Chapter 13. One Syllable Names

When I meet prospective parents, I tend to hear the same question over and over again: "Why aren't there any great one-syllable names for girls?" This chapter answers that question in a fairly conclusive way: there are dozens of excellent names for baby girls that are short, sweet, and just one syllable. A better question - how can you choose just one?

Anne: (Hebrew & Israel): favor or grace
Bea: (America): blessed

Belle: (French): beautiful
Bess: (English): my God is bountiful

Beth: (Scottish): lively
Blair: (Irish & Celtic): from the plain, (Gaelic): child of the fields; (Scottish): peat moss

Blaine: (Gaelic, Irish & Celtic): thin
Blake: (English): pale blond or dark; (Scottish): dark-haired

Bliss: (English): joy, happiness
Blue: (English): the color blue

Blythe: (English): happy
Brea: (French): champion

Bree: (Celtic): broth; (Irish): hill, strong one
Bryce: (Welsh): alert, ambitious

Brie: (French): from the northern region of France
Britt: (Swedish): high goddess

Brooke: (English): lives by the stream
Brynn: (Welsh): hill

Cate: (English): blessed, pure, holy
Cher: (English): beloved

Clove: (German): spice
Cree: (Native American): name of tribe

Dale: (English): valley
Dawn: (English): aurora; (Greek): sunrise

Dove: (American): bird of peace
Drew: (Greek): courageous, strong

Dulce: (Latin): very sweet
Fran/Francine: (Latin America): free

Eve: (Hebrew): to breathe
Faith: (English): faithful; (Latin America): to trust

Fawn: (French & English): young deer
Faye: (French): fairy; (Irish): raven; (English): faith, confidence

Fern: (English): the fern plant
Fleur: (French): flower

Flynn: (Irish): heir to the red-headed
Gayle: (English): merry, lively

Gay: (English): merry, happy
Grace: (Latin America): grace of God; (American): land of grace

Greer: (Scottish): alert, watchful
Gwen: (Celtic): mythical son of Gwastad

Hope: (English): trust, faith
Jade: (Spanish): jewel, green gemstone

Jayne: (Indian): victorious; (Hebrew): gift from God; (English): Jehovah has been gracious
Jean: (Hebrew): God is gracious

Jill: (English): girl, sweetheart
Joan: (Hebrew): gift from God; (English): God is gracious

Joy: (French, English & Latin America): rejoicing
June: (Dominican Republic): born in June

Kate: (Irish, English & French): diminutive of Katherine, which means pure, virginal
Kay: (Greek): rejoice; (Scottish & Welsh): fiery

Kent: (English & Welsh): white; (Celtic): chief
Kim: (Welsh): leader

Kyle: (Irish): attractive
Lane: (English): narrow road, from the long meadow

Lake: (American): body of water, from the lake
Lark: (English): a lark; (American): songbird

Leigh: (English): from the meadow
Liv: (Norwegian): protector

Love: (English): full of affection
Lynn(e): (English): woman of the lake, waterfall

Madge: (English): pearl
Maeve: (Irish): intoxicating, joyous

Maude: (French): strong in war; (Irish): strong battle maiden
Mauve: (American): purplish color

May: (English): name of month; (Hebrew & Latin America): from Mary
Nell: (English): torch

Neve: (Irish): radiant; (Hebrew): life
Noor: (Aramaic): light

Paige: (French): assistant, attendant
Pearl: (English): gemstone

Queen: (English): queen
Quinn: (Celtic): queenly

Rae: (Scottish): grace; (German): wise protection
Rain/Raine: (American): blessings from above; (French & Latin): ruler; (English): lord, wise

Reese: (Welsh): enthusiastic
Rose: (English, French & Scottish): flower, a rose; (German): horse, fame

Rue: (Greek): herb of grace
Ruth: (Hebrew & Israel): companion, friend

Saige/Sage: (English): sage
Scout: (French): scout

Shane: (Hebrew): gift from God; (Irish): God is gracious
Shawn: (Irish): a form of Sean, which means God is gracious

Skye: (English): sky
Sloan: (English): raid; (Irish, Celtic, Scottish & Gaelic): fighter, warrior

Starr: (English & American): star
Tess: (English): harvester

Tish: (Latin): joy
Tyne: (English): of the river Tyne

Vail: (English): valley
Wren: (Welsh): ruler; (English): small bird

Chapter 14. Four-Syllable Names

On a practical basis, this chapter is the flip side of Chapter 13, which presents dozens of one syllable names for girls. Here, we will focus on the longest, most elegant and sophisticated names that are at least four syllables. Why, you may ask, would someone choose this type of name for their child, which is hard to pronounce and spell? Many times, a long name is the best fit for a short and simple last name, such as Smith, Tom, Wu, or Lee. Other times, the parents are seeking a formal name that the child can "grow into," such as Elizabeth. In the meantime, they will call the child one of many possible nicknames, such as Liz, Betty, or Beth.

One fascinating aspect about this list: many of these longer names are older, from other cultures, and not particularly common (with a few notable exceptions). Nevertheless, for parents seeking elegant, sophisticated, and mature names that are also somewhat unusual, this chapter has several hidden gems.

Adelina: (French & Spanish): of the nobility
Alejandra: (Spanish): defender of mankind

Adriana: (Spanish, Greek & Italian): woman with dark and rich features
Alexandra/Alexandria*: (Greek, English & Latin America): defender of mankind

America: (English): ruler of the home
Anastasia: (Greek): resurrection

Angelina: (Italian): little angel
Anjelica: (Greek): a diminutive form of Angela, which means angel

Antonia: (Greek): flourishing or flowering
Apollonia*: (Greek): strength

Aphrodite: (Greek): beauty, love goddess
Arabella: (Latin): answered prayer, beautiful altar

Arianna: (Greek & Italian): holy
Arizona: (Native American): from the little spring, from the state of Arizona

Belisama: (Celtic): goddess of rivers and lakes
Davinia: (Scottish): feminine form of David, which means beloved one

Carolina: (Mexico): beautiful woman; (French & English): song of happiness
Catalina: (Spanish): pure

Caledonia: (Latin): woman of Scotland
Calliope: (Greek): beautiful voice

Cleopatra: (Greek): glory to the father; (African American): queen
Concordia: (Latin): peace

Corinthia: (Greek): woman of Clorinth
Eliana: (Hebrew): the Lord answers our prayers

Elizabeth: (English): my God is bountiful; (Hebrew & Biblical): consecrated to God
Eloisa: (Latin): famous warrior

Emmanuelle: (Hebrew): God is with us
Epiphany: (Greek): manifestation

Ernestina: (German): determined, serious
Esmeralda: (Spanish): resembling a prized emerald

Eugenia: (Greek): well-born
Evangeline: (Greek): like an angel

Fabiana: (Latin): bean grower
Felicity: (French, English & Latin America): happiness

Fidelity: (Latin): faithful, true
Frederica: (German): peaceful ruler

Gabriella: (Israel & Hebrew): God gives strength; (Italian): woman of God
Gardenia: (English): a sweet-smelling flower

Giovanna: (Italian): God is gracious
Guadalupe: (Spanish): from the valley of wolves

Henrietta: (German): ruler of the house
Ileana: (Roman): torch; (Greek): from the city of lion

Isabella: (Hebrew): devoted to God; (Spanish): God is bountiful; (Biblical): consecrated to God
Isadora: (Greek): gift from the goddess Isis

Javiera: (Spanish): owner of a new house
Josephina: (Hebrew): God will add

Julietta: (French): youthful, young at heart
Lavinia: (Latin): purified

Magdalena: (Hebrew): from the tower; (Spanish): bitter
Mahogany: (Spanish): rich, strong

Mariana: (Spanish): star of the sea; (French): bitter
Marietta: (French): star of the sea

Nefertiti: (Egyptian): queenly
Parthenia: (Greek): virginal

Octavia: (Latin America): eighth; (Italian): born eighth
Okalani: (Hawaiian): from the heavens

Olivia: (Spanish & Italian): olive; (Biblical): peace of the olive tree
Olympia: (Greek): from Mount Olympus

Orabella: (Latin): a form of Arabella, which means answered prayer
Oriana: (Latin): born at sunrise

Penelope: (Greek): weaver
Pheodora: (Greek): supreme gift

Philomena: (Greek): friend of strength
Pollyanna: (American): overly optimistic

Seraphina: (Latin): a winged angel
Serenity: (Latin & English): peaceful

Tatiana: (Slavic): fairy queen
Tayanita: (Cherokee): beaver

Theodora: (English): gift of God
Thomasina: (Hebrew): a twin

Tijuana: (Spanish): border town in Mexico
Timothea: (English): honoring God

Valencia: (Spanish & Italian): brave; (Latin America): health or love
Venecia: (Italian): from Venice

Veronica: (Latin): displaying a true image
Victoria: (Latin America): winner

Virgilia: (Latin): staff bearer
Wilhelmina: (German): resolute protector

***Note**: The names Alexandria and Appolonia are five-syllables, rather than four

Chapter 15. Gender Neutral (Unisex) Names

Throughout this book, you have probably stopped at least once or twice and thought: "Wow, I didn't know *that* was a girl's name." To me, that is the most distinctive trend that is worth noting - the fact that few names are reserved for only one sex.

Fifty years ago, that wasn't the case. If you asked someone to suggest a gender neutral name, they would probably say Pat, Lee, Dale, or Frances - and then draw a blank. Now, there are dozens of popular names that are equally used by both sexes. We've included this chapter for two reasons:

1. to offer suggestions for parents who want a gender neutral name

2. to note the names that truly **are** unisex, for prospective parents who might not be aware of this trend. Sadly, I have met several parents who chose a name on this list, thinking that it was exclusively female. A few years later, they were stunned to learn that there were three little boys in their daughter's kindergarten class with the same name.

And, that, ultimately, is the only pitfall of unisex names - they don't "announce" your child's gender the way most conventional names do. Nevertheless, these names are definitely hot and trendy - and well worth a second look.

The Top Unisex Names (with gender divisions) from the 2012 Social Security Administration statistics:

1. **Rowan:** (Irish): red-haired; (English & Gaelic): from the rowan tree (37% female)
2. **Quinn:** (Celtic): queenly; (Gaelic): one who provides counsel (68% female)
3. **Kai:** (American): ocean; (Welsh): keeper of the keys; (Scottish): fire (13% female)
4. **Sawyer**: (English): one who works with wood (17% female)
5. **Charlie**: (English) a diminutive form of Charles, which means strong (41% female)
6. **Avery**: (English): wise ruler (81% female)
7. **Finley**: (Irish): blond-haired soldier (66% female)
8. **Elliott**: (Israel): close to God; (English): the Lord is my God (17% female)
9. **Emery**: (German): industrious (80% female)
10. **Emerson**: (English): brave, powerful (61% female)
11. **Rory**: (Irish): famous brilliance, famous ruler; (Gaelic): red-haired (31% female)
12. **Riley**: (English): from the rye clearing; (Irish): a small stream (59% female)
13. **Marlowe**: (English): from the hill by the lake (88% female)
14. **River**: (Latin & French): stream, water (36% female)
15. **Arden**: (English): passionate, enthusiastic, valley of the eagle (74% female)
16. **Peyton**: (English): from the village of warriors (68% female)
17. **Remy**: (French): oarsman or rower, from Rheims (46% female)
18. **Sage**: (English & French): wise one; (English): from the spice (66% female)
19. **Ellis**: (English & Hebrew): my God is Jehovah (35% female)
20. **Addison**: (English): son of Adam (70% female)

A Comprehensive List of Gender Neutral Names (in alphabetical order)

Addison: (English): son of Adam
Alpha: (Greek): first-born child

Aspen: (English): from the aspen tree
Bailey: (English): bailiff, steward, public official

Blair: (Irish & Celtic): from the plain, (Gaelic): child of the fields; (Scottish): peat moss
Blaine: (Gaelic, Irish & Celtic): thin

Blake: (English): pale blond or dark; (Scottish): dark-haired
Blue: (English): the color blue

Brady: (Irish): a large-breasted woman
Brett: (French, English & Celtic): a native of Brittany

Brice/Bryce: (Welsh): alert, ambitious
Camden/Camdyn: (Irish, Scottish, English & Gaelic): from the winding valley

Cameron: (Irish & Gaelic): crooked nose
Campbell: (Gaelic): crooked mouth; (French): from the beautiful field

Cary/Carey: (Greek): pure
Chris: (English & Irish): follower of Christ

Clancy/Clancey: (Celtic): son of the red-haired warrior
Cleo/Clio: (Greek): to praise, acclaim

Coby/Koby/Kobe: (Hebrew): supplanter
Cody: (English): cushion

Corey/Cory: (Irish): from the hollow, of the churning waters
Dale: (German): valley; (English): lives in the valley

Drew: (Greek): courageous, valiant
Derry: (English, Irish, German & Gaelic): red-haired, from the oak grove

Dakota: (Native American): friend to all
Easton: (English): from east town

Ellison: (English): son of Elias
Ellory/Ellery: (Cornish): resembling a swan

Gale/Gail/Gayle: (English): merry, lively
Flynn: (Irish): heir to the red-head; ruddy complexion

Garnet: (English): gem, armed with a spear; (French): keeper of grain
Gentry: (English): gentleman

Hadley: (English & Irish): from the heath covered meadow
Hagen: (Gaelic): youthful

Halsey: (English): Hal's island
Harlow: (English): from the army on the hill

Harper: (English): one who plays or makes harps
Haven: (English): safe place

Hayden: (English): from the hedged valley
Hunter: (English): hunter

Jai: (Tai): heart
Jamie: (Spanish): supplanter

Jensen: (Scandinavian): God is gracious
Jordan: (Hebrew): to flow down; (Israel): descendant

Kacey/Casey: (Irish): brave
Keaton: (English): from the town of hawks

Kelsey: (English): from the island of ships
Kendall: (English & Celtic): from the bright valley

Kent: (English & Welsh): white; (Celtic): chief
Kennedy: (Gaelic): a helmeted chief

Kerry: (Irish): dark-haired
Kim: (Vietnamese): as precious as gold; (Welsh): leader

Kimball: (Greek): hollow vessel
Kinsey: (English): victorious prince

Kirby: (Scandinavian): church village
Kyle: (Irish): attractive

Laine/Lane: (English): narrow road
Lee/Leigh: (English): meadow

Landon: (English): from the long hill
Linden: (English): from linden hill

London/Londyn: (English): capital of England; fortress of the moon
Lynn(e): (English): waterfall

McKenzie/Mackenzie: (Scottish): son of Kenzie; (Irish): fair, favored one
McKinley: (English): offspring of the fair hero

Mika/Micah: (Finnish): like God; (Japanese): new moon
Monroe: (Gaelic): from the red swamp; (Scottish): from the river; (Irish): near the river roe

Morgan: (Celtic): lives by the sea; (Welsh): bright sea
Murphy: (Irish): sea warrior

O'Shea: (Irish): child of Shea
Orion: (Greek): a hunter in Greek mythology

Page/Paige: (French): youthful assistant
Parker: (English): keeper of the park

Paris: (Persian): angelic face; (Greek): downfall; (French): the capital city of France
Pembroke: (Welsh): headland

Presley: (English): priest's land
Quincy: (English): fifth-born child; (French): estate belonging to Quintus

Rain: (American): blessings from above; (Latin): ruler; (English): lord, wise
Reese/Reece: (English & Welsh): ardent, fiery, enthusiastic

Randy: (German): the wolf shield
Rene/Renee: (French): reborn

Rio: (Spanish & Portuguese): river
Rylan/Ryland: (English): the place where rye is grown

Sailor: (American): sailor
Santana: (Spanish): saintly

Shane: (Hebrew): gift from God; (Irish): God is gracious
Shawn: (Irish): a form of Sean, which means God is gracious

Sheridan: (Irish, English & Celtic): untamed; (Gaelic): bright, a seeker
Shiloh: (Hebrew): he who was sent, God's gift, the one to whom it belongs; (Israel): peaceful

Silver: (English): precious metal, the color silver
Sloan: (English): raid; (Irish, Celtic, Scottish & Gaelic): fighter, warrior

Spencer/Spenser: (English): dispenser of provisions
Storm/Stormy: (English): tempest; (American): impetuous nature

Sydney: (English): wide island
Tai: (Chinese): large; (Vietnamese): prosperous

Teagan: (Gaelic): handsome, attractive
Toby: (Hebrew): God is good

Unique: (Latin): only one; (American): unlike others
Whitley: (English): from the white meadow

Chapter 16. Cultural Preferences: Popular Names for African-American Girls

In a country as large and diverse as the United States, parents often choose baby names that honor their cultural heritage and unique family traditions. By doing so, they bring a depth and richness to our society that is fresh and exciting. Other times, parents choose mainstream names that are equally popular among other racial and ethnic groups. We will explore these trends in this chapter by presenting the most popular names for baby girls in African-American households.

In reading this chapter, please note the source of the data, which prevents us from projecting it to a national level. By design, the Social Security Administration does not break down this information by race; they simply publish the number of times that a name is used across all racial and ethnic groups. Only five states report the information by race: Virginia, Colorado, Arkansas, Texas, and New York. For that reason, we are presenting the top names strictly from those states, in alphabetical order (rather than by popularity). Depending upon where you live - and the level of diversity in your community, these names may (or may not) be particularly common. They do, however, show the amazing range of names that are popular in African-American families in five distinctly different parts of the country.

Aaliyah/Aliyah: (Arabic): an ascender; (Muslim): exalted; (American): immigrant to a new home
Aisha/Aiesha: (African): womanly, lively; (Muslim): life, lively

Alexandra: (Greek, English & Latin America): defender of mankind
Alexis: (English): helper, defender; (Biblical): protector of mankind

Alyssa: (Greek): logical
Amaya: (Japanese & Arabic): night rain

Amber: (Arabic): precious jewel, yellow-brown color
Angel: (Spanish & Greek): angelic

Aniyah: (Polish & Hebrew): God has shown favor
Aretha: (Greek): virtuous

Beyonce: (English & American): one who surpasses others
Brianna: (Irish): strong; (Celtic & English): she ascends

Cambria: (Latin): woman of Wales
Cassandra: (Greek): prophet of doom

Chantal: (French): song
Charmaine: (English): song; (French): beautiful orchard

Cherise: (French): cherry, dear one
Chloe: (Greek): verdant, blooming

Dana: (English, Danish, Irish & Hebrew): a person from Denmark
Davina: (Scottish): feminine form of David, which means beloved one

Dendara: (Egyptian): from the town on the river
Deondra: (American): a combination of Dee and Andrea

Destiny: (English): fate
Diamond: (English): bridge protector; (Greek): unbreakable

Dionne: (Greek): divine queen
Essence: (English): scent

Fawn: (French & English): young deer
Gabrielle: (French): strength of God

Gemma: (French & Italian): jewel
Gwendolyn: (Welsh): fair

Hannah: (English & Hebrew): favor, grace; (Biblical): grace of God
Haylee: (English): from the hay meadow, hero

Imani: (Kenya): faith
Isis: (Egyptian): most powerful goddess

Jada: (Israel): wise
Jacinta: (Spanish): resembling the hyacinth

Jailyn: (American): a combination of Jae and Lynn
Jalisa: (American): a combination of Jae and Lisa

Jasmine: (Persian): a climbing plant; (English): a fragrant flower
Jayla: (Arabia): charity; (African American): one who is special

Jordan: (Hebrew): to flow down; (Israel): descendant
Kayla: (Irish & Greek): pure and beloved

Kennedy: (Gaelic): a helmeted chief
Keisha/Keesha: (African): favorite

Kenya: (Israel): animal horn
Kiara: (Irish): small and dark

Krystal: (American): clear, brilliant glass
Lacrecia: (Latin): bringer of light

Lakeisha: (American): joyful, happy
Lashawna: (American): filled with happiness

Latisha: (Latin): a form of Lucretia, which means bringer of light
Laverne: (French): woodland, like the spring

Layla: (Arabic): beauty of the night
Levona: (Hebrew): spice, incense

Madison: (English): son of Matthew
Makayla: (English & Irish): like God

Marietta: (French): star of the sea
Malia: (American): calm, peaceful

Malika: (African): queen, princess
Nevaeh: (American): gift from God, heaven spelled backwards

Octavia: (Latin America): eighth; (Italian): born eighth
Odessa: (Latin America): the odyssey

Paulina: (Latin America): small
Precious: (American): treasured

Serena: (Latin): peaceful disposition; (African American): calm, tranquil
Sapphire: (Hebrew): sapphire; (Israel): beautiful

Shahina: (Arabic): falcon
Shakila: (Arabic): beautiful one

Shakira: (Arabic): grateful
Shana: (Hebrew): God is gracious

Shandy: (English): rambunctious
Shanelle: (American): a form of Chanel, which means from the canal

Shani: (African): marvelous
Shania: (Native American): on my way

Shanika: (American): a combination of Sha and Nika
Shasta: (Native American): from the triple-peaked mountain

Sheba: (Hebrew): an ancient country in Arabia
Sheena: (Gaelic): God's gracious gift

Sierra: (Spanish): mountain; (Irish): dark
Sydney: (French): from Saint Denis

Talisa/Talissa: (American): consecrated to God
Talisha: (American): damsel, innocent

Tamara: (Hebrew): palm tree; (Israel): spice
Taylor: (English & French): a tailor

Tia: (Greek); princess; (Spanish): princess, aunt; (African American): aunt
Tiana: (Greek): princess

Tiffany: (Greek): lasting love
Trinity: (Latin): the holy three

Xaviera: (Arabic): bright
Yolanda: (Greek): resembling the violet flower

Zakiyyah: (Muslim): sharp, intellectual, pious, pure
Zola: (Mexican): Earth; (French): famous bearer

Chapter 17. Cultural Preferences: Popular Names for Hispanic Girls in the U.S.

On a practical basis, this chapter continues the theme that we started in Chapter 16 - it presents the most popular names for baby girls in Hispanic households in the U.S. (in states that break down this information by race). The selections include a fascinating mix of old and new favorites that blend the richness of the Spanish culture with a decidedly American flair.

In reading this chapter, please note the source of the data, which prevents us from projecting it to a national level. By design, the Social Security Administration does not break down this information by race; they simply publish the number of times that a name is used across all racial and ethnic groups. Only five states report the information by race: Virginia, Colorado, Arkansas, Texas, and New York. For that reason, we are presenting the top names strictly from those states, in alphabetical order (rather than by popularity). Depending upon where you live - and the level of diversity in your community, these names may (or may not) be particularly common. They do, however, show the amazing range of names that are popular in Hispanic families in five distinctly different parts of the country.

Abigail: (Hebrew): father rejoiced; (Biblical): source of joy
Abril: (Spanish): April

Adrianna: (Spanish, Greek & Italian): woman with dark and rich features
Agustina: (Latin America): majestic, grand

Alejandra: (Spanish): defender of mankind
Alexa: (Greek, English & Latin America): defender of mankind

Allison: (English): noble, truthful, strong character
Alma: (Latin & Italian): nurturing, kind

Amalia: (Latin America): industrious; hard working
Amanda: (Latin): much loved

Ana: (Hebrew): favor or grace; (Native American): mother; (Israel): gracious
Andrea: (Greek & Latin): courageous, strong

Antonia: (Greek): flourishing or flowering
Antonella: (Latin America): praiseworthy

Ariana: (Greek & Italian): holy
Bianca: (Italian): white, fair

Camila: (Italian): a noble virgin, a ceremonial attendant
Carla: (Portuguese & Latin America): strong one

Carmella: (Hebrew & Israel): golden; (Spanish): garden
Carolina: (Mexican): beautiful woman; (French & English): song of happiness

Catalina: (Spanish): pure
Clara: (French & Catalonia): clear, bright

Constanza: (American): strong-willed
Corazon: (Spanish): of the heart

Cota: (Spanish): lively
Daniela: (Hebrew & Spanish): God is my judge

Danna: (Indian): gift
Elena: (Spanish): the shining light

Elisa: (Hebrew): my God is bountiful
Emilia: (Spanish): flattering

Emily: (Latin America): admiring
Emma: (English, Danish & German): whole, complete, universal

Fabiana: (Latin): bean grower
Fernanda: (Spanish): adventurous

Filipa: (Spanish): friend of horses
Fiorella: (Italian): little flower

Florencia: (Spanish): flowering, blooming
Gabriella: (Israel & Hebrew): God gives strength; (Italian): woman of God

Guadalupe: (Spanish): from the valley of wolves
Isabella: (Hebrew): devoted to God; (Spanish): God is bountiful; (Biblical): consecrated to God

Isidora: (Spanish): gifted with many ideas
Ivana: (Slavic): God is gracious

Jazmin: (Japanese): the flower
Josefina: (Hebrew): God will add

Jovana: (Spanish): daughter of the sky
Julia: (French): youthful; (Latin America): soft-haired, youthful

Juliana: (Spanish): soft-haired
Julieta: (French): youthful, young at heart

Kiara: (Irish): small and dark
Laura: (English, Spanish & Latin America): crowned with laurel, from the laurel tree

Lola: (Spanish): woman of sorrow
Lucia: (Latin America): bringer of light

Luciana: (Latin America): bringer of light
Luna: (Latin & Latin America): the moon

Magdalena: (Hebrew): from the tower; (Spanish): bitter
Maite: (Spanish): loved

Manuela: (Spanish): God is with us
Maria: (Latin): bitter

Mariana: (French): bitter
Martina: (Latin America): warlike

Mercedes: (Latin): reward, payment; (Spanish): merciful
Mia: (Italian): my; (Biblical): mine

Michelle: (French & Hebrew): like God, close to God
Miranda: (Latin): worthy of admiration

Monserrat: (Latin): jagged mountain
Natalia: (French): to be born at Christmas; (Slovakian): to be born

Nicole: (French): victory of the people
Noa: (Israel): movement

Olivia: (Spanish & Italian): olive; (Biblical): peace of the olive tree
Paloma: (Spanish): dove-like

Paola: (Italian): little
Paula: (Latin America): small

Paulina: (Latin America): small
Rafaella: (Hebrew): healed by God

Regina: (Italian, Spanish & Latin America): queen
Renata: (French): a form of Renee, which means reborn

Romina: (Arabian): from the Christian land
Salome: (Hebrew): peace and tranquility

Samantha: (Hebrew & Biblical): listener of God
Santina: (Spanish): little saint

Sara(h): (Hebrew, Spanish & Biblical): princess
Sofia: (Greek & Biblical): wisdom

Ximena: (Greek): heroine
Valentina: (Spanish & Italian): brave; (Latin America): health or love

Valeria: (French): brave, fierce one; (English): strong, valiant
Valery: (French): brave, fierce one; (English): strong, valiant

Vanessa: (Greek): resembling a butterfly
Victoria: (Latin America): winner

Violeta: (Bulgarian): violet
Zita: (Spanish): little rose

Zoe: (Greek): life, alive

Chapter 18. Popular Names for Asian Twins

In this chapter, we present the most popular names for Asian-American baby girls in the last five years (in states that break down this information by race). These eclectic choices, which reflect the amazing history and culture of China, Japan, and Korea, are intriguing options for parents who seek distinctive first and middle names from a traditional part of the world.

In reading this chapter, please note the source of the data, which prevents us from projecting it to a national level. By design, the Social Security Administration does not break down this information by race; they simply publish the number of times that a name is used across all racial and ethnic groups. Only five states report the information by race: Virginia, Colorado, Arkansas, Texas, and New York. For that reason, we are presenting the top names strictly from those states, in alphabetical order (rather than by popularity). Depending upon where you live - and the level of diversity in your community, these names may (or may not) be particularly common. They do, however, show the amazing range of names that are popular in Asian-American families in five distinctly different parts of the country.

Popular Chinese Names for Girls

Bo: (Chinese): precious
Chun: (Chinese): springtime

Fang: (Chinese): fragrant
Far: (Chinese): flower

Hua: (Chinese): flower
Huan: (Chinese): happiness

Jia: (Chinese): beautiful
Jiao: (Chinese): dainty

Jing: (Chinese): stillness, luxurious
Lan: (Chinese): orchid

Li: (Chinese): upright
Lien: (Chinese): lotus

Lin: (Chinese): resembling jade
Ling: (Chinese): dainty

Meili: (Chinese): beautiful
Mingzhu: (Chinese): bright pearl

Nuo: (Chinese): graceful
Ping: (Chinese): peaceful

Qi: (Chinese): fine jade
Qiang: (Chinese): beautiful rose

Qing: (Chinese): dark blue
Rong: (Chinese): martial

Song: (Chinese): pine tree
Ting: (Chinese): graceful and slim

Xiang: (Chinese): pleasant fragrance
Xiu: (Chinese): grace

Wen: (Chinese): refinement
Yin: (Chinese): silver

Popular Japanese Names for Girls

Aika: (Japanese): love song
Aki: (Japanese): born in autumn

Ame: (Japanese): rain, heaven
Anka: (Japanese): color of the dawn

Fujita: (Japanese): field
Fuyu: (Japanese): born in winter

Hachi: (Japanese): eight, good luck
Haya: (Japanese): quick, light

Kama: (Japanese): one who loves and is loved
Kana: (Japanese): dexterity and skill

Kayo: (Japanese): beautiful
Kenja: (Japanese): a sage

Kin: (Japanese): golden
Kita: (Japanese): north

Ko: (Japanese): filial piety
Kono: (Japanese): dexterity and skill

Kosame: (Japanese): fine rain
Kuma: (Japanese): bear, mouse

Mako: (Japanese): truth, grateful
Mana: (Japanese): truth

Midori: (Japanese): green
Mizuki: (Japanese): beautiful moon

Nami: (Japanese): wave
Naoki: (Japanese): honest tree

Nishi: (Japanese): west
Noriko: (Japanese): child of principles

Raeden: (Japanese): thunder and lightning
Rippina: (Japanese): brilliant light

Sada: (Japanese): pure
Sato: (Japanese): sugar

Sayo: (Japanese): born at night
Shima: (Japanese): true intention

Taka: (Japanese): borrowed
Tama: (Japanese): precious stone

Tomiko: (Japanese): wealthy
Tomoko: (Japanese): two friends

Yukiko: (Japanese): happy child
Yumiko: (Japanese): beautiful and helpful child

Popular Korean Names for Girls

Hae: (Korean): ocean
Hye: (Korean): graceful

Ja: (Korean): attractive, fiery
Ki: (Korean): arisen

Yeo: (Korean): mild
Yon: (Korean): lotus blossom

Chapter 19. Top 10 Names for Girls in Other Countries

Throughout this book, we have focused exclusively on names for baby girls in the United States. For readers with a global perspective, this chapter summarizes the most popular names for girls in *other* countries. In all cases, the data are taken directly from government statistics for that nation (in the last year that data were available). All names are presented in the order of popularity.

Canada (2012)

1. **Olivia:** (Spanish & Italian): olive; (Biblical): peace of the olive tree
2. **Emma:** (English, Danish & German): whole, complete, universal
3. **Sophia:** (Greek & Biblical): wisdom
4. **Emily:** (Latin America): admiring
5. **Ava:** (Latin America): like a bird
6. **Ella:** (English); beautiful fairy; (Spanish): she
7. **Chloe:** (Greek): verdant, blooming
8. **Isabella:** (Hebrew): devoted to God; (Spanish): God is bountiful; (Biblical): consecrated to God
9. **Avery:** (English): counselor, sage, wise
10. **Hannah:** (English & Hebrew): favor, grace; (Biblical): grace of God

Australia (2012)

1. **Ruby:** (English & French): a precious jewel, a ruby
2. **Charlotte:** (French): feminine
3. **Emily:** (Latin America): admiring
4. **Olivia:** (Spanish & Italian): olive; (Biblical): peace of the olive tree
5. **Chloe:** (Greek): verdant, blooming
6. **Amelia:** (English & Latin America): industrious, striving
7. **Mia:** (Italian): my; (Biblical): mine
8. **Sophie:** (Greek & Biblical): wisdom
9. **Isabella:** (Hebrew): devoted to God; (Spanish): God is bountiful; (Biblical): consecrated to God
10. **Ava:** (Latin America): like a bird

Italy (2011)

1. **Sofia:** (Greek & Biblical): wisdom
2. **Giulia:** (Italian): youthful; (Latin America): soft-haired, youthful
3. **Martina**: (Latin America): warlike
4. **Giorgia:** (Italian, Greek & German): farmer
5. **Sara(h):** (Hebrew, Spanish & Biblical): princess
6. **Emma:** (English, Danish & German): whole, complete, universal
7. **Aurora:** (Latin): dawn
8. **Chiara:** (Italian): daughter of the light
9. **Alice:** (Spanish): of the nobility
10. **Alessia:** (Greek): honest

England & Wales (2011)

1. **Amelia:** (English & Latin America): industrious, striving
2. **Olivia:** (Spanish & Italian): olive; (Biblical): peace of the olive tree
3. **Lily/Lilly:** (Hebrew, English & Latin America): lily, blossoming flower
4. **Jessica:** (Israel): God is watching; (Hebrew): rich, God beholds
5. **Emily:** (Latin America): admiring
6. **Sophie:** (Greek & Biblical): wisdom
7. **Ruby:** (English & French): a precious jewel, a ruby

8. **Grace:** (Latin America): grace of God; (American): land of grace
9. **Ava:** (Latin America): like a bird
10. **Isabella:** (Hebrew): devoted to God; (Spanish): God is bountiful; (Biblical): consecrated to God

France (2010)

1. **Emma:** (English, Danish & German): whole, complete, universal
2. **Lea**: (Hebrew): weary
3. **Chloe:** (Greek): verdant, blooming
4. **Manon**: (French): bitter
5. **Ines**: (Spanish): a form of Agnes, which means pure
6. **Lola**: (Spanish): woman of sorrow
7. **Jade**: (Spanish): jewel, green gemstone
8. **Camille**: (Italian): a noble virgin, a ceremonial attendant
9. **Sara(h):** (Hebrew, Spanish & Biblical): princess
10. **Louise**: (German): famous warrior

Spain (2010)

1. **Lucia:** (Latin America): bringer of light
2. **Paula:** (Latin America): small
3. **Maria:** (Latin): bitter
4. **Sara(h):** (Hebrew, Spanish & Biblical): princess
5. **Daniela:** (Hebrew & Spanish): God is my judge
6. **Carla:** (Portuguese & Latin America): strong one
7. **Sofia:** (Greek & Biblical): wisdom
8. **Alba**: (Spanish & Italian): from the city of Alba
9. **Claudia:** (Spanish & Latin America): lame
10. **Martina**: (Latin America): warlike

Ireland (2011)

1. **Emily:** (Latin America): admiring
2. **Sophie:** (Greek & Biblical): wisdom
3. **Emma:** (English, Danish & German): whole, complete, universal
4. **Grace:** (Latin America): grace of God; (American): land of grace
5. **Lily/Lilly:** (Hebrew, English & Latin America): lily, blossoming flower
6. **Sara(h):** (Hebrew, Spanish & Biblical): princess
7. **Lucy:** (Latin America): bringer of light
8. **Ava:** (Latin America): like a bird
9. **Chloe:** (Greek): verdant, blooming
10. **Katie:** (Irish, English & French): diminutive of Katherine, which means pure, virginal

Norway (2012)

1. **Emma:** (English, Danish & German): whole, complete, universal
2. **Nora:** (Hebrew): light
3. **Sofie:** (Greek & Biblical): wisdom
4. **Emilie:** (Latin America): admiring
5. **Ingrid:** (Scandinavian): having the beauty of God
6. **Linnea**: (Denmark): lime tree
7. **Thea:** (Greek): gift of God
8. **Anna:** (Hebrew): favor or grace; (Native American): mother; (Israel): gracious
9. **Amalie:** (French & Latin America): industrious; hard working
10. **Ida**: (English): hardworking

Chapter 20. Names with Similar Meanings

Throughout this book, we have listed the meaning of every name we have presented; we have also provided the same information for each of the 3,000 names in the appendix.

In this chapter, we have summarized a portion of that information for readers who are trying to select a name with a specific meaning. Bear in mind, translations vary widely among languages, which is why we encourage readers to further investigate their top choices, if meanings are important to them. With that in mind, these tables are a general guide to groupings of names that have similar - if not identical - meanings.

Names That Mean "Beautiful or Handsome"

Adina	Alaina	Alanna	Ayanna	Annabella	Arabella
Belinda	Bella	Callie	Calla	Calliope	Calista
Carolina	Carrington	Ella	Inga	Jacinta	Jaffa
Kaelyn	Keely	Lydia	Mabel	Maribel	Maybelline
Meadow	Miyo	Naveen	Neena	Rosalind	Sapphire
Shaina	Shakila	Siri	Serlina	Zaynah	

Names That Mean "Light"

Aileen	Chiara	Eileen	Elaine	Elena	Elani
Ellen	Evelyn	Helen	Helena	Helene	Ilene
Kenzie	Lucile	Lacretia	Letitia	Lucile	Lucinda
Lucy	Ming	Neriah	Nirel	Noor	Nora
Olena	Orle	Rhonwyn	Uriel	Yalena	Yelena
Yitta	Zia	Luka			

Names That Mean "Bitter"

Annmarie	Magdalena	Marianna	Mali	Mara	Maria
Mariah	Marianne	Mariel	Marina	Marissa	Marlie
Marita	Marlene	Maureen	Mary	Meli	Minnie
Mitzi	Moira	Molly	Polly	Romy	

Names That Mean "Strong"

Abira	Allison	Andres	Bree	Brianna	Bridget
Carla	Costanza	Carly	Drew	Ever	Isana
Mahogany	Miriam	Maude	Mena	Megan	Nina
Ondrea	Osita	Plato	Richelle	Valerie	Viveca

Names That Mean "Peace"

Dove	Erin	Fia	Frida	Concordia	Fredericka
Irena	Lana	Malia	Irene	Olivia	Tully
Peace	Ping	Saloma	Serena	Serenity	Shiloh
Winetta	Xerena				

Names That Mean "Noble"

Ada	Adelaide	Adele	Akela	Alberta	Alicia
Alison	Audrey	Camille	Della	Earlene	Elmira
Elsa	Ethyl	Heidi	Trisha	Lyra	Lecia
Marquis	Patricia				

Names That Mean "Bright"

Alanis	Alberta	Candy	Clara	Claire	Clarise
Claudette	Bertha	Electra	Phoebe	Sheridan	Shula
Shirley	Roberta	Ziva	Zahara		

Names That Mean "Brave"

Casey	Tracy	Emerson	Bernadette	Valentina	Valerie
Sloan					

Names That Mean "Warrior"

Eloise	Fiana	Gertrude	Imelda	Katniss	Kimball
Kelly	Murphy	Lois	Louise	Sloan	Trudy

Names That Mean "Dark"

Blake	Bronwyn	Ciara	Maura	Darcy	Delaney
Ebony	Keara	Keri	Layla	Maura	Melanie
Adriana					

Names That Mean "Enlightened or Wise"

Athena	Avery	Freda	Jada	Medora	Minerva
Monique	Ophelia	Rae	Rain	Ramona	Rayna
Sage	Ulima				

Names That Mean "Red"

Auburn	Clancy	Crimson	Derry	Flynn	Flann
Flynn	Scarlett	Sienna	Reed	Rooney	Rory
Rowan	Omri	Phoenix			

Names That Mean "Fiery"

Edana	Flame	Reese	Seraphina	Keegan	McKenna
McKayla					

Names That Mean "Gift from God"

Dita	Dora	Dorothea	Eudora	Dorothy	Isadora
Jane	Joan	Janice	Janine	Joanna	Juanita
Neveah	Pheodora	Shea	Shane	Sheena	Shiloh
Shona	Shonda	Siobhan	Theodora		

Names That Mean "(God is) Gracious"

Anais	Anita	Anna	Annette	Annika	Elisha
Gia	Gianna	Giovanna	Jeanette	Ivana	Ivanka
Jana	Janae	Janelle	Janessa	Janice	Jeanne
Jane	Jean	Jeannette	Joann	Jensen	Jonna
Nanette	Shana	Shane	Shawn	Sheena	Winola

Names That Mean "Protector/Defender"

Alexandria	Alexis	Alexi	Alejandra	Liv	Meredith
Ramona	Sasha	Sandrine	Shura	Sandra	Xantata
Willa					

Names That Mean "Champion or Victorious"

Kinsey	Brea	Jane	Tori	Nia	Neela
Nikita	Eunice	Victoria	Sigourney	Collette	

Names That Mean "Joy or Happy"

Abigail	Beatrice	Joy	Bliss	Carolyn	Hillary
Edith	Jovi	Jovita	Jubilee	Lakeisha	Ranita
Merry	Rona	Tatum	Tisha	Olina	Rowena
Blythe	Bunny	Felicia	Jocelyn	Nara	Gay

Names Relating "To The Sea"

Bela	Chelsea	Cordelia	Delores	Doris	Galilee
Ionia	Mariah	Mali	Marin	Mariana	Marietta
Marianne	Marika	Marina	Marissa	Maris	Maureen
Meredith	Muriel	Meryl	Morgan	Ula	Umiko
Narelle	Narissa	Pasha	Sula		

Names That Mean "Sun"

Asia	Dawn	Eldora	Kalina	Helene	Kira
Liane	Roxanne	Oriana	Sunshine	Solana	Sorina
Surya	Zelene	Zelia	Zora		

Names That Mean "Queen"

Cleopatra	Dionne	Juno	Latanya	Malika	Nala
Nefertiti	Quintana	Queen	Quinn	Raine	Rani
Regina	Reina	Reya	Thema	Tania	Tatiana
Thelma	Tonia	Quinn			

Names That Mean "Star"

Astra	Danica	Vega	Estelle	Esther	Hester
Spica	Quarralia	Vespera	Star	Stella	

Names That Mean "Consecrated to God"

Bettina	Elizabeth	Isabella	Talisa	Lisa	Liza

Chapter 21. Names that Sound Alike

Many times, parents disagree on a potential name for superficial reasons:

- it is too popular
- the initials don't work
- their sister, best friend, or cousin is planning to use the same name
- a bad connotation (i.e., the name elicits memories of a professional rival, childhood bully, or former romantic partner)

Often, the solution to this dilemma is choosing a name that *rhymes* with the original - it has a similar sound and feel, without the negative "baggage." This chapter presents several combinations of girls' names that rhyme. If you like one - but you can't persuade your partner to choose it, see if (s)he likes the other........

Anna/Ana: (Hebrew): favor or grace; (Native American): mother; (Israel): gracious
Hannah: (English & Hebrew): favor, grace; (Biblical): grace of God

Bella: (Hebrew): devoted to God; (Spanish & Latin America): beautiful
Ella: (English); beautiful fairy; (Spanish): she
Stella: (French, Italian & Greek): star

Darcy: (Irish & Celtic): dark one
Marcy: (Latin America): marital

Kayla: (Irish): pure and beloved
Jayla: (Arabia): charity; (African American): one who is special
Layla: (Indian): born at night; (Arabian): dark beauty
Shayla: (Irish): her gift

Cara: (Celtic): friend; (Italian & Dominican Republic): dear, beloved
Mara: (English, Italian, Hebrew & Israel): bitter
Sara(h): (Hebrew, Spanish & Biblical): princess
Tara: (Irish & Scottish): a hill where the kings meet; (Irish): tower, hillside

Carla: (Portuguese & Latin America): strong one
Marla: (Greek): high tower

Candy: (American): bright, sweet; (Hebrew): famous bearer
Mandy: (Latin America): worthy of love
Sandy: (English): a diminutive for of Sandra, which means unheeded prophetess

Chloe: (Greek): verdant, blooming
Zoe (or Zoey): (Greek): life, alive

Ellen: (Greek): light
Helen: (Greek): light

Kiley: (Irish): narrow land
Riley/Rylee: (Irish): a small stream

Flynn: (Irish): heir to the red-headed
Lynn(e): (English): waterfall
Quinn: (Celtic): wise; (Irish): fifth, counsel, intelligent

Jayne: (Indian): victorious; (Hebrew): gift from God; (English): Jehovah has been gracious
Rain/Raine: (American): blessings from above; (French & Latin): ruler; (English): lord, wise
Blaine: (Gaelic, Irish & Celtic): thin

Callie: (Greek): beautiful; (English); lark
Tally: (Irish): surname

Addison: (English): son of Adam
Madison: (English): son of Matthew

Minnie: (Irish): bitter; (Hebrew): wished for a child
Winnie: (Irish & Celtic): white, fair

Clarissa: (Spanish & Italian): clear; (Latin America): brilliant
Alyssa: (Greek): logical
Melissa: (Greek): honey bee
Marissa: (Latin America): of the sea; (Hebrew): rebellion, bitter

Marilyn: (Israel): descendants of Mary
Carolyn: (English): joy, song of happiness

Valerie: (French): brave, fierce one; (English): strong, valiant
Mallory: (French): unfortunate; ill-fated; (German): war counselor

Hailey/Hailee/Haley: (English): hero, field of hay
Kaylee: (American): pure
Bailey: (English): bailiff, steward, public official

Jess: (Israel): wealthy
Tess: (English): harvester
Bess: (Hebrew, English & Israel): oath of God, God is satisfaction

Molly: (Israel & English): bitter
Holly: (French, English & Germany): shrub
Polly: (Latin America): bitter
Dolly: (America): cute child

Sherry: (Israel): beloved; (French): dear one
Merry: (English): merry, joyous

Laura: (English, Spanish & Latin America): crowned with laurel, from the laurel tree
Maura: (Italian, Irish & French): dark
Dora: (Greek): gift

Tia: (Greek); princess; (Spanish): princess, aunt; (African American): aunt
Lia: (Greek): bearer of good news
Mia: (Italian): my; (Biblical): mine
Nia: (Irish): champion
Pia: (Italian): devout
Gia: (Italian): God is gracious

Nina: (Hebrew); grace; (Spanish): girl; (Native American): strong
Tina: (English): river
Gina: (Italian): garden; (African American): powerful mother of black people
Dina: (Hebrew & Israel): avenged, judged; (English): from the valley

Gay: (English): merry, happy
Rae: (Scottish): grace; (Germany): wise protection
Fay: (French): fairy; (Irish): raven; (English): faith, confidence
Kay: (Greek): rejoice; (Scottish & Welsh): fiery
May: (English): name of month; (Hebrew & Latin America): from Mary

Stacy: (English): productive, resurrection
Tracy: (English): brave
Casey: (Celtic & Gaelic): brave; (Irish): observant, alert, brave; (Spanish): honorable
Macy: (English): enduring; (American): stone worker
Lacy: (Irish): surname; (English): derived from lace
Gracie: (English & Latin America): grace

Irene: (Greek & Spanish): peaceful
Eileen: (Irish & French): light
Colleen: (Irish & Gaelic): girl
Darlene: (English & French): little darling
Marlene: (Germany): bitter; (Hebrew): from the tower
Sharlene: (English & French): manly, from the name Charles

Appendix: Alphabetical List of Girls Names

Aaliyah/Aliyah: (Arabic): an ascender; (Muslim): exalted; (American): immigrant to a new home
Abby/Abbey/Abby: (Hebrew): diminutive form of Abigail, which means father rejoiced
Abena: (African): born on a Tuesday
Abiela: (Hebrew): my father is Lord
Abigail: (Hebrew): father rejoiced; (Biblical): source of joy
Abira: (Hebrew): strong
Abra: (Hebrew): mother of many nations
Abril: (Spanish): April
Ada: (English): wealthy; (Hebrew): ornament; (German): noble; (African): first daughter
Addison: (English): son of Adam
Adelaide: (French & German): noble, kind
Adelina/Adeline: (French & Spanish): of the nobility
Adell/Adele: (German & French): noble, kind
Adina: (Israel): beautiful; (Hebrew): slender
Adriana/Adrianna: (Spanish, Greek & Italian): woman with dark and rich features
Afra: (Hebrew): young doe
Afton: (English): from the Afton River
Agatha: (Latin & Greek): pure, virtuous, good
Agnes: (Greek): pure
Agustina: (Latin America): majestic, grand
Aika: (Japanese): love song
Aileen: (Irish): light bearer, from the green meadow
Ainsley: (Scottish): one own's meadow
Aisha/Aiesha: (African): womanly, lively; (Muslim): life, lively
Aiyanna/Aiyana/Aianna: (Native American): forever flowering
Aja: (Indian): goat
Akela: (Hawaiian): noble
Aki: (Japanese): born in autumn
Akilah: (Arabic): intelligent
Akira: (Scottish): anchor
Alaina: (French): dear child, beautiful and fair woman
Alana: (Irish): beautiful, peaceful
Alanis: (English): attractive and bright
Alba: (Spanish & Italian): from the city of Alba
Alberta: (German & French): noble and bright
Alejandra: (Spanish): defender of mankind
Alessia: (Greek): honest
Alexandria/Alessandra/Alexa/Alexandra: (Greek, English & Latin America): defender of mankind
Alexi: (English): helper, defender
Alexis: (English): helper, defender; (Biblical): protector of mankind
Ali: (Arabian): noble, sublime
Alice/Alyce: (Spanish): of the nobility
Alicia/Alysha: (English): of noble birth; (Spanish & German): sweet
Aline: (Dutch): alone; (Celtic & Irish): fair, good looking
Allegra: (Latin): cheerful
Allison/Alison: (English): noble, truthful, strong character
Alma: (Latin & Italian): nurturing, kind
Almira: (Arabic): aristocratic
Alpha: (Greek): first-born
Althea: (Greek): wholesome, healer
Alyssa: (Greek): logical
Amalia/Amalie: (French & Latin America): industrious; hard working
Amanda: (Latin): much loved

Amaranth: (Greek): an unfading flower
Amaya: (Japanese & Arabic): night rain
Amber: (Arabic): precious jewel, yellow-brown color
Ambra: (French): jewel; (Italian): Amber color
Ambrosia: (Greek): immortal
Ame: (Japanese): rain, heaven
Amelia: (English & Latin America): industrious, striving
America: (English): ruler of the home
Amethyst: (Greek): wine, a purple gemstone
Amira: (Arabic): princess
Amrita: (Hindu): nectar of eternal immortality
Amy/Aimee: (English, French & Latin America): beloved
Anais: (Hebrew): gracious
Anastasia: (Greek): resurrection
Anat: (Hebrew & Israel): a singer
Andrea: (Greek & Latin): courageous, strong
Andrina: (English): courageous, valiant
Angel: (Spanish & Greek): angelic
Angela: (Spanish, French, Italian & Latin America): angel
Angelina: (Italian): little angel
Angelique: (Greek): heavenly messenger
Anita: (Italian, Hebrew & Latin America): gracious
Aniyah: (Polish & Hebrew): God has shown favor
Anja: (Russia): grace of God
Anjelica: (Greek): a diminutive form of Angela, which means angel
Anka: (Japanese): color of the dawn
Anna/Ana: (Hebrew): favor or grace; (Native American): mother; (Israel): gracious
Annabel/Annabelle: (Italian): graceful and beautiful
Annabeth: (English): graced with God's bounty
Annalynn: (English): from the graceful lake
Anne: (Hebrew & Israel): favor or grace
Annette: (French & Hebrew): gracious
Annika: (Dutch): gracious
Annmarie: (English): filled with bitter grace
Anona: (English): pineapple
Antonia: (Greek): flourishing or flowering
Antonella: (Latin America): praiseworthy
Antoinette: (French): flowering; (Latin): praiseworthy
Anya: (Russian): graced with God's favor
Anyssa/Anissa: (English): a form of Agnes, which means pure
Aphrodite: (Greek): beauty, love goddess
Apollonia: (Greek): strength
Apple: (America): sweet fruit
April: (English): opening buds of spring; (Latin America): opening, fourth month
Arabella: (Latin): answered prayer, beautiful altar
Arden: (English): passionate, enthusiastic, valley of the eagle
Aretha: (Greek): virtuous
Aria: (Italian): melody
Arianna/Ariana: (Greek & Italian): holy
Ariel/Arial: (Hebrew): lioness of God
Arista: (Latin): harvest
Arizona: (Native American): from the little spring, from the state of Arizona
Arlene/Arleen: (Irish): pledge
Artemis: (Greek): goddess of the moon

Ashanti: (African): great African woman
Ashley: (English & Biblical): lives in the ash tree
Ashlyn: (American): combination of Ashley and Lynn
Asia: (Greek & English): resurrection, rising sun
Aspen: (English): from the aspen tree
Astra: (Latin): of the stars
Astraea: (Greek): justice
Astrid: (Scandinavian & German): divine strength
Athena: (Greek): wise, goddess of wisdom and war
Aubrey: (English): one who rules with elf-wisdom
Audrey: (English): noble strength
Audrina: (English): nobility, strength
Augusta: (Latin): venerable, majestic
Aura: (Greek): soft breeze: Latin: golden
Aurora: (Latin): dawn
Autumn: (English & Latin America): the fall season
Ava: (Latin America): like a bird
Avalon: (Latin): island
Avery: (English): counselor, sage, wise
Avril: (English); born in April
Ayanna: (Hindi & African): innocent, resembling a beautiful flower
Azura/Azure: (Persian): a blue, semi-precious stone

Babette: (French & German): a diminutive form of Barbara, which means stranger
Bailey: (English): bailiff, steward, public official
Bambi: (Italian): child
Barbara: (Latin America): stranger
Bathsheba: (Hebrew): oath, voluptuous, famous bearer; (Biblical): seventh daughter
Bea: (American): blessed
Beatrice: (Italian): blessed; (French): bringer of joy
Bebe: (Spanish): a diminutive form of Barbara, which means stranger
Becca: (Hebrew): a diminutive form of Rebecca, which means tied or bound
Bela: (Slovakian): she of fair skin; (Indian): sea shore; (Hebrew): destruction
Belinda: (English): beautiful and tender woman
Belisama: (Celtic): goddess of rivers and lakes
Bella: (Hebrew): devoted to God; (Spanish & Latin America): beautiful
Belle: (French): beautiful
Bernadette: (French): brave as a bear
Bernadine: (English & German): brave as a bear
Bernice: (French & Greek): one who brings victory
Bertha: (Germany): bright
Beryl: (Greek & English): green jewel
Bess: (English): my God is bountiful
Beth: (Scottish): lively
Bethany: (Hebrew & Israel): a life-town near Jerusalem
Bettina: (English): consecrated to God
Beulah: (Hebrew & Israel): married
Beverly: (English): beaver field
Beyonce: (American): one who surpasses others
Bianca: (Italian): white, fair
Bibi: (Latin): lively
Bijou: (French): as precious as a jewel
Billie: (English): desire to protect
Blaine: (Gaelic, Irish & Celtic): thin
Blair: (Irish & Celtic): from the plain, (Gaelic): child of the fields; (Scottish): peat moss
Blake: (English): pale blond or dark; (Scottish): dark-haired

Bliss: (English): joy, happiness
Blossom: (English): fresh, flowerlike
Blue: (English): the color blue
Blythe: (English): happy
Bo: (Chinese): precious
Bonnie: (English): good; (French): sweet; (Scottish): pretty, charming
Brady: (Irish): a large-breasted woman
Brande/Brandy/Brandie: (English): a woman wielding a sword, an alcoholic drink
Branwen: (Welsh): raven
Brea: (French): champion
Bree: (Celtic): broth; (Irish): hill, strong one
Brenda: (Gaelic): little raven; (Scandinavian): sword
Brenna: (Welsh): like a raven
Brianna/Breanna: (Irish): strong; (Celtic & English): she ascends
Brice/Bryce: (Welsh): alert, ambitious
Bridget/Brigid: (Irish): strong and protective
Brie: (French): from the northern region of France
Bristol: (English): bridge
Britt/Britta: (Swedish): high goddess
Brittany: (English & Celtic): from Britain
Bronte: (Greek): thunder
Bronwyn: (Welsh): dark and pure; (English): white-skinned
Brooke: (English): lives by the stream
Brooklyn: (English): water, stream
Brynn: (Welsh): hill
Buffy: (American): buffalo, from the plains
Bunny: (Greek): a diminutive form of Beatrice, which means blessed, happy
Burgundy: (French): a region of France that is famous for its wine

Caden: (English): battle maiden
Cadence: (Latin): rhythmic and melodious
Cady: (American): happiness
Cairo: (African): the Egyptian city
Caitlyn/Kaitlyn: (Irish): pure
Caledonia: (Latin): woman of Scotland
Callie/Cally: (Greek): beautiful; (English); lark
Calliope: (Greek): beautiful voice
Calista: (Greek): most beautiful
Calla: (Greek): resembling a lily, beautiful
Cambria: (Latin): woman of Wales
Camdyn: (English): of the enclosed valley
Cameo: (Italian): sculptured jewel; (English & Latin America): a shadow or carved gem portrait
Cameron/Camryn: (Irish & Gaelic): crooked nose
Camila/Camilla/Camille: (Italian): a noble virgin, a ceremonial attendant
Campbell: (Scottish): crooked mouth
Candace: (English): pure, glittering white
Candida: (Latin): white-skinned
Candy/Candi: (American): bright, sweet; (Hebrew): famous bearer
Canisa: (Greek): much-loved
Cantrelle: (French): song
Caprice: (Italian): fanciful
Caprina: (Italian): from the island Capri
Cara: (Celtic): friend; (Italian & Dominican Republic): dear, beloved
Carey: (Irish): pure; (Celtic): from the fortress
Cari: (Latin America): beloved

Carina: (Latin): little darling
Carissa/Caressa: (Greek): woman of grace
Carla: (Portuguese & Latin America): strong one
Carleen/Carlene: (English): derivative of Caroline, which means song of happiness
Carlessa: (American): restless
Carlie/Carly: (American): strong one; (Latin America): little, womanly
Carlotta: (Italian): a derivative of Charlotte, which means feminine
Carmel: (Hebrew): garden; (Israel): woodland; (Celtic): from the vineyard
Carmela/Carmella: (Hebrew & Israel): golden; (Spanish): garden
Carmen: (English): garden; (Spanish & Latin America): song
Carnie: (Latin): vocal
Carol: (French): melody, song
Carolina/Caroline: (Mexican): beautiful woman; (French & English): song of happiness
Carolyn: (English): joy, song of happiness
Carrie: (American): melody, song
Carrington: (English): beautiful
Carys: (Welsh): one who loves and is loved
Casey/Cacie/Kasey: (Celtic & Gaelic): brave; (Irish): observant, brave; (Spanish): honorable
Casia: (English): alert, vigorous
Cassandra: (Greek): prophet of doom
Cassidy: (Irish): curly-haired
Catalina: (Spanish): pure
Cate: (English): blessed, pure, holy
Catherine: (English): pure, virginal
Cathleen/Kathleen: (Irish): a form of Catherine/Katherine, which means pure, virginal
Cayenne: (French): hot and spicy
Cayla: (American): crowned with laurel
Caylee: (American): crowned with laurel
Ceara: (Irish): a derivation of Ciara, which means dark-skinned
Cecilia: (Latin): blind
Cecily/Cicely: (Latin): a form of Cecilia, which means blind
Celeste: (Latin): heavenly daughter
Celia: (Italian): heavenly
Celina/Celine: (Latin): of the heavens
Cera: (French): colorful woman
Cerise: (French): cherry
Chai: (Israel & Hebrew): life
Chakra: (Arabic): center of spiritual energy
Chalice: (French): goblet
Chambray: (French): a lightweight fabric
Chanda: (Sanskrit): enemy of evil
Chandelle: (French): candle
Chandra: (Hindi): of the moon
Chanel: (French): from the canal, a channel
Chantal/Chantel: (French): song
Chantrise: (French): a singer
Charisma: (Greek): grace
Charity: (English): kindness, generous, goodwill
Charlaine: (English): feminine form of Charles, which mean manly
Charlize: (French): manly
Charlotte: (French): feminine
Charmaine: (English): song; (French): beautiful orchard
Chastity: (Latin): pure
Chelsea: (English): seaport
Chen: (China): great, dawn
Cher: (English): beloved

Cherise/Cherice/Cherisse: (French): cherry, dear one
Cherish: (English): to be held dear, values
Cherry: (French): dear one; America: cherry
Cheryl/Sheryl: (English): beloved
Chesney: (English): one who promotes peace
Cheyenne: (French): dog; (Native American): an Algonquin tribe
Chiara: (Italian): daughter of the light
China: (Chinese): fine porcelain
Chiquita: (Spanish): little one
Chloe: (Greek): verdant, blooming
Christina/Christine/Christal/Christa/Chrissy: (English): follower of Christ
Chun: (Chinese): springtime
Ciara: (Irish): dark beauty
Cierra: (Spanish): dark-skinned
Cilla: (Latin): sturdy, vision
Cinderella: (French & English): of the ashes
Cinnamon: (American): reddish-brown spice
Clancy/Clancey: (American): light-hearted
Clara: (French & Catalonia): clear, bright
Clarabelle: (French & Catalonia): clear, bright/(French): beauty
Clare/Clair/Claire: (English): clear; (French): bright
Clarice: (French): famously bright
Clarissa: (Spanish & Italian): clear; (Latin America): brilliant
Claudia/Claudine: (Spanish & Latin America): lame
Claudette: (Spanish): a form of Clara, which means clear, bright
Clementine: (French): merciful
Cleo/Clio: (English); father's glory
Cleopatra: (Greek): glory to the father; (African American): queen
Cloris: (Greek): goddess of flowers
Clove: (German): spice
Clover: (English): meadow flower
Coby: (Hebrew): supplanter
Cody: (English): cushion
Colleen: (Irish & Gaelic): girl
Collette: (English): victorious people
Concordia: (Latin): peace
Constanza/Constance/Connie: (American): strong-willed
Consuela: (Spanish): provides consolation
Contessa: (Italian): a countess
Cora: (Greek & English): maiden; (Scottish): seething pool
Coral: (English): a reef formation
Corazon: (Spanish): of the heart
Cordelia: (English, Welsh & Celtic): of the sea
Coretta: (Greek): a form of Cora, which means maiden
Corey/Cory: (Irish): from the hollow, of the churning waters
Corina: (Latin): spear-wielding woman
Corinthia: (Greek): woman of Clorinth
Cornelia: (Latin): horn
Cota: (Spanish): lively
Cote: (French): from the riverbank
Courtney: (English): courteous
Cree: (Native American): name of tribe
Cressida: (Greek): golden girl
Crimson: (English): deep red color
Crystal/Krystal: (English): jewel; (Latin America): a clear brilliant glass

Cyan: (American): light blue or green
Cylee: (American): darling daughter
Cynthia: (Greek): moon
Cyrene: (Greek): maiden huntress

Dagmar: (Scandinavian): born on a glorious gay
Dahlia: (Swedish): from the valley, resembling the flower
Daisy: (English); day's eve; (American): daisy flower
Dakota: (Native American): friend, ally, tribal name
Dale: (English): valley
Dalia/Dahlia: (Hebrew): tree branch
Dana: (English, Danish, Irish & Hebrew): a person from Denmark
Dania: (English, Hebrew & Denmark): God is my judge
Danica: (Slavic): the morning star
Daniela: (Hebrew & Spanish): God is my judge
Danielle: (Hebrew): God is my judge
Danna: (Indian): gift
Daphne: (Greek): of the laurel tree
Dara: (Hebrew): compassionate
Darby: (Irish & Gaelic): free man; (English): deer park
Darcy: (Irish & Celtic): dark one
Daria: (Greek): wealthy
Darlene: (English & French): little darling
Davena/Davina/Davinia: (Scottish): feminine form of David, which means beloved one
Davon: (English): river
Dawn: (English): aurora; (Greek): sunrise
Dea: (Greek): resembling a goddess
Deana/Deanna: (English & Latin America): from the valley
Deborah: (Hebrew & Israel): honey bee
Deidre: (Gaelic): a raging or broken-hearted woman
Dekla: (Latvian): a trinity goddess
Dela/Della: (German, Greek & English): noble
Delaney: (Irish): dark challenger; (French): from the elder-grove tree
Delia: (Greek): visible
Delilah: (Hebrew): a seductive woman
Delora/Delores/Deloris: (Latin America): of the seashore; (English): sorrow
Delta: (Greek): from the mouth of the river, the fourth letter of the Greek alphabet
Demeter: (Greek): lover of the earth
Demi: (Greek): a petite woman; (French): half
Dena: (Hebrew & Israel): vindicated; (Native American): valley
Denali: (Indian): a superior woman
Dendara: (Egyptian): from the town on the river
Denise: (French): a follower of Dionysus
Deondra/Deandra: (American): a combination of Dee and Andrea
Derry: (English, Irish, German & Gaelic): red-haired, from the oak grove
Desiree: (French): desired
Destiny: (English): fate
Deva: (Hindi): divine
Devin/Devon: (Irish): poet
Dextra: (Latin): skillful
Dharma: (Indian): ultimate law of all things
Diamond: (English): bridge protector: (Greek): unbreakable
Diana: (Greek): divine, goddess of the moon and the hunt
Diane: (Latin America): hunter
Dina: (Hebrew & Israel): avenged, judged; (English): from the valley
Dinah: (Hebrew & Israel): judgment

Dionne: (Greek): divine queen
Dita: (Spanish): a form of Edith, which means gift
Dixie: (American): woman of the south
Dolly: (American): cute child
Dolores: (Spanish): woman of sorrow
Dominique: (French): belonging to God
Donna: (Italian): lady
Dora/Dori/Dory: (Greek): gift
Doreen: (French): golden one; (Gaelic): brooding
Doris: (Greek): sea
Dorothea: (Dutch): gift of God
Dorothy (Greek): gift of God
Dove: (American): bird of peace
Drucilla/Drusilla: (Biblical): fruitful, dewy-eyed; (Latin America): mighty
Drew: (Greek): courageous, strong
Drury: (French): greatly loved
Dulce: (Latin): very sweet

Earlene: (Irish): pledge; (English): noble
Eartha: (English): earthy
Easter: (American): from the holiday or Christian festival
Easton: (American): wholesome
Ebony: (American): dark strength
Echo: (Greek): sound returned
Edana: (Irish): fiery
Eden: (Hebrew): delight; (Israel): paradise
Edie: (English): blessed
Edith: (English): joyous, a treasure
Edna: (Celtic): fire; (Hebrew): rejuvenation; (Israel): spirit renewed
Edwina: (English): prosperous friend
Effie: (Greek): melodious talk
Eileen: (Irish & French): light
Elaine: (French): light
Elana: (Hebrew): from the oak tree
Elata: (Latin): high spirited
Eldora: (Spanish): golden, blond, gift of the sun
Eleanor/Elinor: (English): torch
Electra: (Greek): bright, the shining one
Elena: (Spanish): the shining light
Eleni: (Greek): light
Eliana: (Hebrew): the Lord answers our prayers
Elisa/Elise: (Hebrew): my God is bountiful
Elisha: (Hebrew): God is salvation; (Israel): God is gracious
Eliza: (French): consecrated to God
Elizabeth: (English): my God is bountiful; (Hebrew & Biblical): consecrated to God
Ella: (English); beautiful fairy; (Spanish): she
Elle: (English): torch
Ellen/Ellyn: (Greek): light
Ellery: (English): cheerful
Ellie: (English): a diminutive form of Ellen, which means light
Elliott: (Israel): close to God; (English): the Lord is my God
Ellis: (English & Hebrew): my God is Jehovah
Elma: (German): having God's protection
Elmira: (English): noble
Eloisa/Eloise: (Latin): famous warrior
Elrica: (German): great ruler

Elsa: (German): noble
Elsie: (English): my God is bountiful
Elvira: (Latin): truthful, trusted
Emerald: (English, Spanish & French): a bright green gem
Emerson: (English): brave, powerful
Emery: (German): industrious
Emilia: (Spanish): flattering
Emily: (Latin America): admiring
Emma: (English, Danish & German): whole, complete, universal
Emmanuelle: (Hebrew): God is with us
Emme: (Latin America): industrious, striving
Emmylou: (American): universal ruler
Enid: (Welsh): life, spirit
Enya: (Scottish): jewel, blazing
Epiphany: (Greek): manifestation
Erica: (Denmark): honorable ruler
Erin: (Irish): peace
Ernestina/Ernestine: (German): determined, serious
Esme: (French): esteemed
Esmeralda: (Spanish): resembling a prized emerald
Essence: (English): scent
Estelle: (French & Latin America): star
Esther: (Hebrew & Africa): star
Estrella: (Spanish): star
Ethyl: (English): noble
Etta: (German): little
Eudora: (Greek): honored gift
Eugenia: (Greek): well-born
Eunice: (Greek): happy, victorious
Eva: (Hebrew, Israel, Indian & Spanish): one who gives life
Evangeline: (Greek): like an angel
Eve: (Hebrew): to breathe
Evelyn: (Celtic): light; (English & Hebrew): life, hazelnut
Ever: (English): strong as a boar
Evita: (Spanish): a derivative of Eve, which means to breathe

Fabiana: (Latin): bean grower
Faith: (English): faithful; (Latin America): to trust
Faline: (Irish): in charge
Fallon: (Irish): a commanding woman
Fang: (Chinese): fragrant
Far: (Chinese): flower
Fantasia: (Latin): from a fantasy land
Farren: (English): wanderer
Fatima: (Arabic): the perfect woman
Fauna: (French): fawn, a young deer
Fawn: (French & English): young deer
Fay/Faye: (French): fairy; (Irish): raven; (English): faith, confidence
Felicia/Felice/Phylicia: (French & Latin America): happiness
Felicity: (French, English & Latin America): happiness
Fern: (English): the fern plant
Fernanda: (Spanish): adventurous
Fia: (Portuguese): weaver; (Italian): from the flickering fire; (Scottish): from the dark of peace
Fiana: (Irish): warrior huntress
Fidelity/Fidealia: (Latin): faithful, true
Filipa: (Spanish): friend of horses

Fina: (English): God will add
Finley: (Gaelic): fair-haired, heroine
Fiona: (Gaelic): fair, a white-shouldered woman
Fiorella: (Italian): little flower
Flair: (English): natural talent
Flame: (American): passionate, fiery
Fleta: (English): swift
Fleur: (French): flower
Flora: (English): flower: (Latin): flowering
Florence: (English): flowering; (Latin America): prosperous
Florencia: (Spanish): flowering, blooming
Flynn: (Irish): heir to the red-head; ruddy complexion
Fortuna: (Latin): fortunate
Fran/Francine: (Latin America): free
Frances: (Latin America): free
Francesca: (Italian): one who is free
Freda/Freida: (German): wise judge
Frederica: (German): peaceful ruler
Freira: (Spanish): sister
Freya: (Norse): lady
Frida: (German): peaceful
Fujita: (Japanese): field
Fuschia: (Latin): resembling the color
Fury: (Greek): an enraged woman
Fuyu: (Japanese): born in winter

Gabriella: (Israel & Hebrew): God gives strength; (Italian): woman of God
Gabrielle: (French): strength of God
Gail/Gale/Gayle: (English): merry, lively
Galiana: (Arabic): a Moorish princess
Galilee: (Hebrew): from the sacred sea
Gardenia: (English): a sweet-smelling flower
Garnet: (English): gem, armed with a spear; (French): keeper of grain
Gay: (English): merry, happy
Gemma: (French & Italian): jewel
Genesis: (Hebrew): origin, birth; (Israel): beginning
Geneva: (French): juniper berry: (German): of the race of woman
Genevieve: (French): white-skinned
Genia/Genie: (Greek): well-born
Gentry: (English): gentleman
Georgette/Georgeann/Georgeanna/Georgina: (French): farmer
Georgia: (Greek & German): farmer
Geraldine: (English): mighty with a spear
Germaine: (French): from Germany
Gertrude: (German): adored warrior
Gia: (Italian): God is gracious
Giada: (Italian): jade
Gianna: (Italian): diminutive form of Giovanna, which means God is gracious
Gillian/Jillian: (English): child of the gods; (Irish): young at heart
Gina/Geena: (Italian): garden; (African American): powerful mother of black people
Ginger: (English): the spice
Giovanna: (Italian): God is gracious
Giselle: (French): pledge
Gita: (Hindi): beautiful song; (Hebrew): good woman
Gitana: (Spanish): gypsy

Giulia/Giuliana: (Italian): youthful
Gladys: (Welsh): lame
Glenna: (Gaelic): from the valley between the hills
Gloria: (Latin): renowned, highly praised
Glynnis: (Welsh): from the valley between the hills
Golda/Goldie: (English): resembling the precious metal
Grace/Gracie: (Latin America): grace of God; (American): land of grace
Greer: (Scottish): alert, watchful
Greta: (German): pearl
Gretchen: (German): a form of Margaret, which means pearl
Gretel: (German & Scandinavian): pearl
Guadalupe: (Spanish): from the valley of wolves
Guinevere: (Celtic): white lady; (English): white wave
Gwen: (Celtic): mythical son of Gwastad
Gwendolyn: (Welsh): fair
Gwyneth: (Welsh): blessed with happiness
Gypsy: (English): wanderer

Hachi: (Japanese): eight, good luck
Hadley: (English): from the field of heather
Hae: (Korean): ocean
Hagan: (Irish): youthful
Hagar: (Hebrew): forsaken, flight, famous bearer; (Israel): flight
Hailey/Hailee/Haley/Haylee: (English): hero, field of hay
Haimi: (Hawaiian): one who searches for the truth
Hallie/Halle: (English): hay meadow
Halsey: (American): playful
Hana: (Japanese): flower; (Arabic): blissful
Hannah: (English & Hebrew): favor, grace; (Biblical): grace of God
Hara: (Hebrew): from the mountainous land
Harley: (English): from the meadow of the hares
Harlow: (American): impetuous
Harmony: (Latin America): a beautiful blending
Harper: (English): musician, harp player
Harriet: (English & German): rules the home
Hattie: (English): a form of Harriet, which means rules the home
Haven: (English): safe place
Haya: (Japanese): quick, light
Hayden: (English): from the hedged valley
Haylee: (English): from the hay meadow, hero
Hazel: (English & Irish): the hazel tree
Heather: (English): a flowering plant
Heaven: (American): from the heavens
Hedda/Hedy: (German): battler
Heidi: (German): noble, serene
Helen: (Greek): light
Helena: (Greek): light
Helene: (French): in the light of the sun
Helga: (German): wealthy, blessed
Heloise: (French): famous in battle
Henrietta: (German): ruler of the house
Hera: (Greek): Goddess of marriage
Hermione: (Greek): earthly
Hermona: (Hebrew): from the mountain peak
Herra: (Greek): daughter of the earth
Hester: (Greek): star

Hestia: (Greek): goddess of the hearth
Hilary/Hillary: (English & Greek): joyous, cheerful
Hilda: (German): battle maiden
Hoda: (Indian): child of God
Holly: (French, English & Germany): shrub
Honey: (English): sweet
Honor: (Spanish & Irish): honor; (Latin America): integrity
Hope: (English): trust, faith
Hua: (Chinese): flower
Huan: (Chinese): happiness
Hunter: (English): hunter
Hye: (Korean): graceful

Ida: (English): hardworking
Idona: (Scandinavian): fresh-faced
Ilaina/Ilana: (Hebrew): tree
Ileana: (Roman): torch; (Greek): from the city of lion
Ilene: (Irish): a form of Helen, which means light
Ilia: (Greek): from the ancient city
Ilsa: (German): abbreviation of Elizabeth, which means God is bountiful
Imala: (Native American): one who disciplines others
Iman: (Arabic): having great faith
Imani: (Kenya): faith
Imari: (Japanese): daughter of today
Imelda: (Italian): warrior
Imogene: (Latin): image, likeness
Ina: (Polynesian): moon goddess
Inara: (Arabic): heaven-sent daughter
Inari: (Finnish): successful, woman from the lake
Inca: (Indian): adventurer
India: (English): from India
Indigo: (Latin America): dark blue
Indira: (Hindi): splendid
Ineesha: (American): sparkling
Inez/Ines: (Spanish): a form of Agnes, which means pure
Inga: (Danish & Swedish): beautiful daughter
Ingrid: (Scandinavian): having the beauty of God
Inis: (Irish): woman from Ennis
Iona: (Greek): woman from the island
Ionanna: (Hebrew): filled with grace
Ionia: (Greek): of the sea and islands
Ipsa: (Indian): desired
Ireland: (Irish): country of the Irish
Irena: (Greek): peace
Irene: (Greek & Spanish): peaceful
Iris: (Greek): colorful, rainbow; (Hebrew & English): the flower
Irma: (German): whole, universal
Isabel: (Hebrew): devoted to God; (Spanish & Biblical): consecrated to God
Isabella: (Hebrew): devoted to God; (Spanish): God is bountiful; (Biblical): consecrated to God
Isadore/Isadora: (Greek): gift from the goddess Isis
Isana: (German): strong willed
Ishtar: (Arabic): mythical goddess of love and fertility
Isidora: (Spanish): gifted with many ideas
Isis: (Egyptian): most powerful goddess
Isla: (Greek & Irish): from the island
Isra: (Arabic): one who travels in the evening

Ivana: (Slavic): God is gracious
Ivanka: (Slavic): God is gracious
Ivette/Yvette: (French): a form of Yvette, which means young archer
Ivory: (English & Latin America): white, pure
Ivy/Ivey: (English): vine

Ja: (Korean): attractive, fiery
Jacey/Jacy/Jacie: (American): resembling the hyacinth
Jacinda: (Greek): beautiful
Jacinta: (Spanish): resembling the hyacinth
Jacqueline: (French): to protect
Jada/Jayda: (Israel): wise
Jade: (Spanish): jewel, green gemstone
Jae: (English): resembling a jaybird
Jael: (Hebrew): mountain goat, climber
Jaffa: (Hebrew): beautiful
Jai: (Tai): heart
Jaiden: (Spanish): a form of Jade, which means jewel
Jailyn: (American): a combination of Jae and Lynn
Jalila: (Arabic): important
Jalisa: (American): a combination of Jae and Lisa
Jamaica: (American): from the island of springs
Jamie/Jayme: (Hebrew): supplanter
Jamielee: (American): a combination of Jamie and Lee
Jamielynn: (American): a combination of Jamie and Lynn
Jana: (Slovakian): God is gracious
Janae: (American): a form of Jane, which means gracious
Jane: (Hebrew): gift from God; (English): gracious, merciful
Janelle/Jeanelle: (French): a form of Jane, which means gracious
Janesha/Janessa: (American): a form of Jane, which means gracious
Janet: (Hebrew & English): gift from God
Janice/Janis: (Hebrew): gift from God; (Israel): God is gracious
Janine: (Hebrew): gift from God
January: (American): the first month of the year
Jasmine: (Persian): a climbing plant; (English): a fragrant flower
Javiera/Xaviera: (Spanish): owner of a new house
Jayla: (Arabia): charity; (African American): one who is special
Jayne: (Indian): victorious; (Hebrew): gift from God; (English): Jehovah has been gracious
Jazmin: (Japanese): the flower
Jean: (Hebrew): God is gracious
Jeanette: (French): a derivative of Jean, which means God is gracious
Jeanne: (Scottish): a form of Jean, which means God is gracious
Jemima: (Hebrew): our little dove
Jemma: (English): as precious as a jewel
Jena/Jenna: (Arabic): our little bird
Jennifer: (English & Welsh): fair one; (English & Celtic): white wave
Jensen: (Scandinavian): God is gracious
Jeri/Jerri/Jerrie: (American): diminutive forms of Geraldine, which means mighty with a spear
Jerica: (American): a combination of Jeri and Erica
Jermaine: (French): woman from Germany
Jessica: (Israel): God is watching; (Hebrew): rich, God beholds
Jetta: (Danish): resembling the gemstone
Jewel/Jewelle: (English & French): precious gem
Jezebel: (Hebrew): one who is not exalted
Jia: (Chinese): beautiful
Jiao: (Chinese): dainty

Jiera: (Lithuanian): lively
Jill: (English): girl, sweetheart
Jillian/Gillian: (English): child of the gods; (Irish): young at heart
Jinelle: (Welsh): fair skin
Jing: (Chinese): stillness, luxurious
Jiselle: (American): one who offers her pledge
Jo: (English): God will add
Joan: (Hebrew): gift from God; (English): God is gracious
Joann: (English & Hebrew): God is gracious
Joanna: (Hebrew & French): gift from God
Joba/Joby: (Hebrew): afflicted
Jobeth: (American): a combination of Jo and Beth
Jocelyn/Josslyn/Josselin: (Latin): cheerful, happy
Joda: (Hebrew): an ancestor of Christ
Jody: (Hebrew): praised
Joelle: (Hebrew): God is willing
Jolene/Joleen/Joline: (English): God will add
Jolie: (French): pretty young woman
Jonna/Johnna: (Danish): God is gracious
Jordan/Jordana: (Hebrew): to flow down; (Israel): descendant
Jorja: (English): farmer
Josephina/Josefina: (Hebrew): God will add
Josephine: (French): God will add
Josette: (French): a form of Josephine, which means God will add
Journey: (American): one who likes to travel
Jovana/Jovanna: (Spanish): daughter of the sky
Jovi/Jovita: (Spanish): joyful
Joy: (French, English & Latin America): rejoicing
Joyce: (English & Latin America): cheerful, merry
Juana/Juanita: (Spanish): a form of Jane, which means gift from God
Jubilee: (Latin): joyous celebration
Judith/Judy/Judi: (Hebrew): praised; (Israel): from Judah
Julia/Julie: (French): youthful; (Latin America): soft-haired, youthful
Juliana: (Spanish): soft-haired
Juliet/Juliette: (French): youthful, soft-haired
Julietta/Julieta: (French): youthful, young at heart
June: (Dominican Republic): born in June
Juno: (Roman): mythical queen of the heavens
Justina: (Greek): just
Justine: (English): just, upright; (Latin America): fairness

Kacey/Casey: (Irish): brave
Kacia: (Greek): the adoptive mother of Romulus and Remus
Kady/Katy: (American): a diminutive form of Katherine, which means pure or virginal
Kaelin/Kaylin/Kaelyn: (American): a combination of Kay and Lynn; (Irish): beautiful girl from the meadow
Kaia: (Greek): earth
Kailani: (Hawaiian): sky
Kaitlyn/Caitlyn/Katelyn/Catelyn: (Irish): pure
Kala: (Hawaiian): princess
Kalina/Kaleena/Kalena: (Indian): of the sun
Kallan: (Slavic): stream, river
Kama: (Indian & Japanese): one who loves and is loved
Kamala: (Hawaiian, Hindu & Indian): lotus; (Arabic): perfection
Kami: (Hindu): loving; (Japanese): divine aura
Kamila: (Czechoslovakian): young ceremonial attendant
Kana: (Japanese): dexterity and skill

Kanda: (Native American): a magical woman
Kara: (Greek): pure; (Italian): dearly loved; (Gaelic): a good friend
Karen: (Greek): pure
Kari: (Norwegian): blessed, pure, holy
Karina/Kareena/Karena/Carina/Carena/Careena: (Scandinavian & Russian): dear one, pure
Karisma/Charisma: (English): blessed with charm
Karissa: (Greek): grace, kindness
Karla: (German): a small and strong woman
Karmel: (Latin): of the fruitful orchard
Kasia: (English): alert, vigorous
Kate: (Irish, English & French): diminutive of Katherine, which means pure, virginal
Katherine/Kathryn: (Irish): clear; (English): pure; (Greek): pure, virginal
Kathleen/Kathy: (English, Irish & French): diminutive of Katherine, which means pure
Katniss: (American): female warrior
Katrina: (German): a form of Katherine, which means pure
Kay: (Greek): rejoice; (Scottish & Welsh): fiery
Kayden: (French, English & Arabic): round, gentle; companion
Kayla: (Irish & Greek): pure and beloved
Kaylee/Kayleen/Kaylene: (American): pure
Kayo: (Japanese): beautiful
Keagan/Keegan: (Irish): little, fiery
Keara: (Irish): dark, black
Kearney: (Irish): the winner
Keaton: (English): from a shed town
Keely/Keeley: (Irish): beautiful
Keilani: (Hawaiian): glorious chef
Keira: (Celtic): black-haired
Keisha/Keesha: (African): favorite
Kelly/Kelli/Kelleigh/Kellee: (Gaelic & Irish): warrior; (Scottish): wood
Kelsey: (English): from the island of ships
Kendall: (English & Celtic): from the bright valley
Kendra: (English): having royal power
Kenja: (Japanese): a sage
Kennedy: (Gaelic): a helmeted chief
Kent: (English & Welsh): white; (Celtic): chief
Kenya: (Israel): animal horn
Kenzie: (Scottish): light-skinned; (American): diminutive of McKenzie
Keri/Kerry: (Irish): dusky, dark
Ki: (Korean): arisen
Kiara: (Irish): small and dark
Kiera: (Irish): dusky
Kiley: (Irish): narrow land
Kim: (Vietnamese): as precious as gold; (Welsh): leader
Kimball: (English): chief of warriors
Kimberlin/Kimberlyn: (English): a form of Kimberly, which means ruler
Kimberly: (English): ruler
Kimora: (American): royal
Kin: (Japanese): golden
Kina: (Hawaiian): woman of China
Kinley: (American): diminutive of McKinley
Kinsey: (English): the king's victory
Kira: (Russian): sun
Kirby: (Scandinavian): church village
Kirsten: (Greek): Christian, annointed
Kismet: (English): fate
Kita: (Japanese): north

Kitty: (Greek): a diminutive form of Katherine, which means pure, virginal
Ko: (Japanese): filial piety
Kobe/Kobi/Koby: (African): supplanter; (American): from California
Komala: (Indian): tender and delicate
Kona: (Hawaiian): girly
Kono: (Japanese): dexterity and skill
Kosame: (Japanese): fine rain
Kris/Kristen/Kristi/Krista: (Irish): Christ-bearer
Kristina/Kristine: (English): follower of Christ
Krystal: (American): clear, brilliant glass
Kuma: (Japanese): bear, mouse
Kyla: (English): from the narrow channel
Kyle: (Irish): attractive
Kylee: (Celtic): a straight and narrow channel
Kylie: (Australian): a boomerang
Kyra: (Greek): noble

Lacrecia/Lacresha/Lucretia: (Latin): bringer of light
Lacy/Lacey: (Irish): surname; (English): derived from lace
Laila/Leila/Leyla: (Arabic): beauty of the night
Laine/Lane/Lainey/Laney/Lanie: (English): narrow road, from the long meadow
Lake/Laken/Lakin/Lakyn: (American): body of water, from the lake
Lakeisha: (American): joyful, happy
Lalita: (Indian): playful and charming
Lan: (Chinese): orchid
Lana: (Latin): wooly; (Irish): attractive, peaceful
Lanassa: (Russian): cheerful, lighthearted
Landon: (English): from the long hill
Lani: (Hawaiian): from the sky, heavenly
Laquita: (American): fifth-born child
Lara: (Greek): cheerful; (Latin): shining, famous
Laramie: (French): shedding tears of love
Larissa/Laryssa/Laurissa: (Greek): cheerful
Lark: (English): a lark; (American): songbird
Larue: (American): a medicinal herb
Lashawna: (American): filled with happiness
Lata: (Indian): of the lovely wine
Latanya: (American): daughter of the fairy queen
Latisha/Leticia/Letitia: (Latin): a form of Lucretia, which means bringer of light
Latoya: (American): a combination of La and Toya
Laura: (English, Spanish & Latin America): crowned with laurel, from the laurel tree
Laurel: (English & French): crowned with laurel, from the laurel tree
Lauren/Laryn/Lauryn: (French): crowned with laurel
Laurie/Lori: (English): crowned with laurels
Lavender: (English): a purple flowering plant
Laverne: (French): woodland, like the spring
Lavina/Lavinia: (Latin): purified
Layla/Leila(h): (Indian): born at night; (Arabian): dark beauty
Layne: (English): path, roadway
Leah/Leia: (Hebrew): weary
Leann: (English): gracious meadow
Lecia: (English): noble, truthful
Leda: (Greek): mother creator
Leeza: (Hebrew & English): a form of Lisa, which means devoted to God
Leigh: (English): from the meadow
Leighton: (English): herb garden, town by the meadow

Leila/Leyla: (Persian): night, dark beauty
Leilani: (Hawaiian): heavenly flower, heavenly child
Lena: (Israel): illustrious
Lenora/Lenore/Leora: (Greek & Russian): a form of Eleanor, which means torch
Leona: (Latin): strength of a lion
Leslie/Lesley: (Gaelic): from the holly garden
Leta: (Latin): glad
Leticia: (Spanish): joy, gladness
Levin: (Hebrew): heart; (English): dear friend
Levona: (Hebrew): spice, incense
Lexa/Lexia: (Czech): defender of mankind
Li: (Chinese): upright
Lia: (Greek): bearer of good news
Liane/Liana: (English): daughter of the sun
Libby: (English): my God is bountiful
Liberty: (English): free, independent
Libra: (Latin): balanced, the seventh sign of the zodiac
Lien: (Chinese): lotus
Lila: (Arabia): night
Lilac: (Latin America): bluish purple; (American): a flowering bluish purple shrub
Lilith: (Babylonian): woman of the night
Lillian: (Latin): resembling the lily
Lilo: (American): generous one
Lily/Lilly: (Hebrew, English & Latin America): lily, blossoming flower
Lin: (Chinese): resembling jade
Lina: (Arabic): tender
Linda: (Spanish): pretty; (English): lime tree; (German): snake, lime tree
Linden: (English): from linden hill
Lindley: (English): from the pasture land
Lindsay/Lindsey/Lyndsay/Lyndsey: (English): from the land of linden trees
Linette/Lynette: (Welsh): idol; (French): bird
Ling: (Chinese): dainty
Linnea: (Denmark): lime tree
Lisa: (German): devoted to God; (Israel): consecrated to God
Lisette/Lissettte/Lizette: (French): derivation of Elizabeth, which means my God is bountiful
Liv: (Norwegian): protector
Livia: (English): life
Liza: (Hebrew): consecrated to God
Lois: (Israel): good; (German): famous warrior
Loki: (Norse): a trickster god in mythology
Lola: (Spanish): woman of sorrow
Lolita: (Spanish): sorrowful
Lona/Loni: (English): ready for battle
London/Londyn: (English): capital of England; fortress of the moon
Lora: (Latin): crowned with laurel
Lorelei: (German): from the rocky cliff
Loretta: (Italian): crowned with laurel
Lori: (English) the laurel tree; (Latin America): crowned with laurel
Lorita: (Latin America): laurel
Lorraine: (French): from the kingdom of Lothair
Lotus: (Greek): the flower
Louise/Louisa: (German): famous warrior
Love: (English): full of affection
Luana/Luann: (Hawaiian): contented
Lucile: (English): a form of Lucy, which means bringer of light
Lucinda: (Latin): a form of Lucy, which means bringer of light

Lucrecia: (Spanish): brings light
Lucy/Lucia/Luciana: (Latin America): bringer of light
Luka: (Latin America): bright
Lulu: (Arabic): pearl; (English): soothing
Luna: (Latin & Latin America): the moon
Lupe/Lupa/Lupita: (Latin): wolf
Lurleen/Lurlene: (Scandinavian): war horn
Lydia: (Greek): beautiful maiden
Lyla/Lila: (Arabic): born at night
Lynn(e): (English): waterfall
Lyric: (Greek): melodic word; (French): of the lyre
Lysandra: (Greek): liberator
Mabel: (English): lovable, beautiful
Mackenna: (Gaelic): daughter of the handsome man
Mackenzie/Mackinsey: (Irish & Scottish): fair, favored one
Macy: (English): enduring; (American): stone worker
Maddox: (English): born into prosperity
Madeline/Madelyn: (Greek): high tower
Madge: (English): pearl
Madison: (English): son of Matthew
Madonna: (Italian): my lady
Maeve: (Irish): intoxicating, joyous
Magdalena: (Hebrew): from the tower; (Spanish): bitter
Maggie: (English): resembling a pearl
Magnolia: (French): resembling the flower
Mahogany/Mahogony: (Spanish): rich, strong
Maia: (French): May; (Greek): mother
Maisie: (Scottish): resembling a pearl
Maite: (Spanish): loved
Makala: (English): princess; (Hawaiian): resembling myrtle
Makayla: (English & Irish): like God
Makena: (African): filled with happiness
Mako: (Japanese): truth, grateful
Mali: (Thai): resembling a flower; (Welsh): from the sea of bitterness
Malia (American): calm, peaceful
Malika: (African): queen, princess
Mallory/Malerie: (French): unfortunate; ill-fated; (German): war counselor
Mamie: (American): a diminutive form of Margaret, which means pearl
Mana: (Japanese): truth
Mandy: (Latin America): worthy of love
Manon: (French): bitter
Manuela: (Spanish): God is with us
Mara: (English, Italian, Hebrew & Israel): bitter
Marcela/Marcella: (Spanish): warring
Marcia/Marsha: (Latin): dedicated to Mars
Marcy: (Latin America): marital
Maren/Marin: (Latin): sea
Margaret: (Greek & Latin America): a pearl
Mari: (Finnish): bitter
Maria/Marie: (Latin): bitter
Mariah: (English): bitter; (Latin): star of the seas
Mariana/Marian: (Spanish): star of the sea; (French): bitter
Marianne/Marian: (French): bitter; (Spanish): star of the sea
Maribel: (French): beautiful
Mariel: (Hebrew): bitter
Marietta: (French): star of the sea

Marika: (Danish): star of the sea
Marjorie/Margery: (English): resembling a pearl
Marlie/Marley/Marleigh/Marly: (American): bitter
Marlo: (English): one who resembles driftwood
Marilyn/Marlyn: (Israel): descendants of Mary
Marina: (Greek, Italian & Slovakian): from the sea
Maris: (Latin): sea
Marissa: (Latin America): of the sea; (Hebrew): rebellion, bitter
Marita: (Dutch): bitter
Marla: (Greek): high tower
Marlene: (German): bitter; (Hebrew): from the tower
Marlowe: (English): from the hill by the lake
Marnie/Marny: (Hebrew): rejoice
Marquesa: (Spanish): she who works with a hammer
Marquise: (French): noble woman
Marsala: (Italian): from the place of sweet wine
Martha: (Israel): lady
Martina: (Latin America): warlike
Mary: (Biblical, English & Slovakian): bitter
Matilda: (German): powerful battler
Maude: (French): strong in war; (Irish): strong battle maiden
Maura: (Italian, Irish & French): dark
Maureen: (Irish): star of the sea, from the sea of bitterness
Mauve: (American): purplish color
Maven: (English): having great knowledge
Mavis: (French): resembling a songbird
Maximiliana: (Latin): eldest
Maxine/Maxie: (Latin): greatest
May/Mae: (English): name of month; (Hebrew & Latin America): from Mary
Maya/Mya: (Indian): an illusion or dream; (Hebrew): woman of the water
Maybelline: (Latin): a form of Mabel, which means lovable, beautiful
McKayla: (Gaelic): fiery
McKenzie: (Irish): fair, favored one
McKinley: (English): offspring of the fair hero
Meadow: (American): beautiful field
Meagan/Megan: (Irish): soft and gentle; (Greek): strong and mighty
Medea: (Greek): cunning ruler
Medina: (Arabic): the site of Muhammad's tomb
Medora: (Greek): wise ruler
Medusa: (Greek): a Gorgon with snakes for hair
Megara: (Greek): wife of Hercules
Meili: (Chinese): beautiful
Melanie: (Greek): dark-skinned beauty
Melba: (Greek): slender, thin-skinned
Meli: (Native American): bitter
Melia: (German): industrious
Melika: (Greek): as sweet as honey
Melina: (German): industrious, striving
Melinda: (Latin): sweet and gentle
Melissa: (Greek): honey bee
Melita: (Greek), a form of Melissa, which means honey bee
Melody: (Greek): beautiful song
Melora: (Greek): golden apple
Mena: (German & Dutch): strong
Mercedes: (Latin): reward, payment; (Spanish): merciful
Mercy: (English): compassion; (French): merciful

Meredith: (Welsh): great ruler, protector of the sea
Merrilee: (American): a combination of Merry and Lee
Merry: (English): joyful, mirthful
Meryl: (German): famous; (Irish): shining sea
Mia: (Italian): my; (Biblical): mine
Michaela: (Celtic, Hebrew, English, Gaelic & Irish): who is like God
Michelle: (French & Hebrew): like God, close to God
Midori: (Japanese): green
Mika/Micah: (Finnish): like God; (Japanese): new moon
Mikala/Mikaela: (Hawaiian): who is like God
Mila: (Russian): dear one; (Serbian): favor, glory
Mildred: (English): gentle counselor
Miley: (American): virtuous
Millicent: (English): industrious
Mimi: (French): a diminutive form of Miriam, which means rebellious
Mindy: (English): sweet and gentle
Minerva: (Latin): wise
Ming: (Chinese): brilliant light
Mingzhu: (Chinese): bright pearl
Minka: (Teutonic): great strength
Minnie: (Irish): bitter; (Hebrew): wished for a child
Mira: (Hindu): prosperous
Mirabel: (Spanish): of uncommon beauty
Miranda: (Latin): worthy of admiration
Miriam: (Hebrew): rebellious; (Israel): strong-willed
Mischa: (Russian): like God
Misty: (English): shrouded by mist
Mitzy/Mitzi: (German): diminutive form of Mary, which means bitter
Miya: (Japanese): from the sacred temple
Miyo: (Japanese): beautiful daughter
Mizuki: (Japanese): beautiful moon
Moesha: (American): drawn from the water
Moira: (Irish): bitter
Molly: (Israel & English): bitter
Mona: (Gaelic): born into nobility
Monica: (Greek & Spanish): advisor
Monique: (French): one who provides wise counsel
Monroe: (Gaelic): from the red swamp; (Scottish): from the river; (Irish): near the river roe
Monserrat: (Latin): jagged mountain
Montana: (Latin America): mountainous
Morgan: (Celtic): lives by the sea; (Welsh): bright sea
Morgana: (Welsh & Celtic): dweller of the sea
Mulan: (Chinese): magnolia blossom
Muriel: (Arabian): myth; (Celtic): shining sea
Murphy: (Irish): sea warrior
Mya: (American): emerald
Myka: (Hebrew): who is like God
Myra: (Greek): fragrant
Myrina: (Latin): an amazon in mythology
Myrtle: (Greek): the tree, victory; (English): the flowering shrub

Nadia: (Slovakian): hopeful
Nadine: (French): hopeful; (German): the courage of a bear
Nadira: (Arabic): rare, precious
Nailah/Naila: (Arabic): successful
Nala: (African): successful; (Tanzanian): queen

Nami: (Japanese): wave
Nan: (English): gracious
Nana: (Hawaiian): born in the spring
Nancy: (Hebrew & English): grace
Nandita: (Indian): delightful daughter
Nanette: (English): favor; (French & Hebrew): gracious
Naoki: (Japanese): honest tree
Naomi: (Hebrew & Israel): pleasant
Nara: (Greek): happy; (English): north; (Japanese): oak
Narella: (Greek): intelligent
Narelle: (Australian): woman from the sea
Nari: (Japanese): thunder
Narissa/Narcissa: (Greek): dafodil
Natalia/Natalie: (French): to be born at Christmas; (Slovakian): to be born
Natasha: (Greek): rebirth
Naveen: (Hindu): new; (Irish): beautiful, pleasant
Navida: (Iranian): brings good news
Nazareth: (Hebrew): religion
Neda: (Slovakian): Sunday's child; (English): wealthy guardian
Neena: (Hindi): beautiful eyes
Nefertiti: (Egyptian): queenly
Neila/Neela/Neely: (Irish): champion
Nelle/Nelly: (English): torch
Nena: (English): girl
Neriah: (Israel): light lamp of the Lord
Nerissa: (Italian): black-haired beauty; (Greek): sea nymph
Nessa: (Hebrew): miracle child; (Greek): pure, chaste
Neta: (Hebrew): plant, shrub
Neva: (Spanish): covered with snow
Nevada: (English): covered in snow
Nevaeh: (American): gift from God, heaven spelled backwards
Neve: (Irish): radiant; (Hebrew): life
Nevena: (Irish): worshipper of the saint
Neylan: (Turkish): fulfilled wish
Nia: (Irish): champion; (African): purpose
Nicole: (French): victory of the people
Nicolette: (French): a form of Nicole, which means victory of the people
Nikita: (Russian): victorious people
Nila: (Indian): blue
Nina: (Hebrew); grace; (Spanish): girl; (Native American): strong
Nirel: (Hebrew): light of God
Nishi: (Japanese): west
Nissa: (Hebrew): sign, emblem
Nita: (Hebrew): planter; (Choctaw): bear
Noa: (Israel): movement
Noelle: (French): born at Christmastime
Nola: (Irish): champion
Nona: (English): ninth
Noor: (Aramaic): light
Nora/Norah: (Hebrew): light
Noriko: (Japanese): child of principles
Norleen: (Irish): honest
Norma: (Latin America): from the north
Nuala: (Irish): white, fair-shouldered
Nula: (Irish): white: shouldered

Nuna: (Native American): land
Nuo: (Chinese): graceful
Nyala: (African): resembling an antelope
Nyssa: (Greek): the beginning

O'Shea: (Irish): child of Shea
Oba: (Yoruba): chief, ruler
Ocean/Oceana: (Greek): ocean
Octavia: (Latin America): eighth; (Italian): born eighth
Odelia: (Greek): melodic
Odessa: (Latin America): the odyssey
Odette: (German & French): a form of Odelia, which means melodic
Odina: (Latin): from the mountain
Okalani: (Hawaiian): from the heavens
Oksana: (Russian): hospitality
Ola: (Nigerian): precious; Scandinavian: ancestor
Oleda: (English): resembling a winged creature
Olena: (Russian): a form of Helen, which means light
Olethea: (Latin): truthful
Olga: (Slovakian): holy
Oliana: (Polynesian): oleander
Olina: (Hawaiian): joyous
Oliva: (Latin): olive tree
Olive: (Irish): olive; (Latin America), olive branch, peace
Olivia: (Spanish & Italian): olive; (Biblical): peace of the olive tree
Olympia: (Greek): from Mount Olympus
Oma: (Hebrew): reverent
Omri: (Arabic): red-haired
Ona: (Hebrew): grace
Ondrea: (Slavic): courageous and strong
Onida/Oneida: (Native American): the one expected
Onyx: (Greek): the onyx stone
Oona: (Gaelic): pure, chaste
Opal: (English & Indian): precious gem
Ophelia: (Greek): useful, wise
Ophrah/Oprah: (Hebrew): resembling a fawn
Orabella: (Latin): a form of Arabella, which means answered prayer
Oriana: (Latin): born at sunrise
Orin: (Latin): dark-haired beauty
Orion: (Greek): huntress
Orla: (Irish): golden woman
Orli: (Hebrew): light
Orna/Ornice: (Irish): pale skinned
Ornat: (Irish): green
Ornella: (Italian): of the flowering ash tree
Orpah: (Israel): fawn
Osaka: (Japanese): from the city of industry
Osita: (Spanish) divinely strong
Overton: (English): from the upper side of town
Ozora: (Hebrew): wealthy

Padma: (Hindi): lotus
Paige: (French): assistant, attendant
Paloma: (Spanish): dove-like
Pamela: (Greek, English & Indian): honey
Pandora: (Greek): gifted and talented woman

Paola: (Italian): little
Parker: (English): keeper of the park
Paris: (Persian): angelic face; (Greek): downfall; (French): the capital city of France
Parthenia: (Greek): virginal
Pasha: (Greek): sea
Patience: (English): patient, enduring
Patricia: (Spanish & Latin America): noble
Patrina/Patrice: (American): born into nobility
Paula/Paulette: (Latin America): small
Pauline/Paulina: (Latin America): small
Peace: (English): peaceful
Peaches: (English): fruit
Pearl: (English): gemstone
Pembroke: (English): from the broken hill
Penelope: (Greek): weaver
Penny: (Greek): diminutive form of Penelope, which means weaver
Peony: (Greek): resembling the flower
Pepita: (Spanish): God will add
Perdita: (Latin): lost
Peri: (Persian): fairy; (English); from the pear tree
Perlita: (Italian): pearl
Peta: (Blackfoot): golden eagle
Petra/Petrina/Petrisse: (Greek & Latin): small rock
Petunia: (English): resembling the flower
Peyton: (English): village
Pheodora: (Greek): supreme gift
Phernita: (American): well-spoken
Phia: (Italian): saintly
Philana: (Greek): lover of mankind
Philippa/Pippa: (English): friend of horses
Philomena: (Greek): friend of strength
Phoebe: (Greek): bright, shining one
Phoenix: (Greek): dark-red color, an immortal bird
Phylicia/Felicia: (Latin): fortunate, happy
Phyllis: (Greek): green leaf
Pia: (Italian): devout
Pilar: (Spanish): pillar of strength
Ping: (Chinese): peaceful
Piper: (English): plays the flute
Pippi: (French): friend of horses; (English): blushing
Pita: (African): fourth daughter
Pixie: (English): mischievous fairy
Plato: (Greek): strong shoulders
Plena: (Latin): abundant, complete
Polina: (Russian): small
Polly: (Latin America): bitter
Pollyanna: (American): overly optimistic
Poloma: (Choctaw): bow
Pomona: (Latin): goddess of fruit trees
Poppy: (English & Latin America): the poppy flower
Portia/Porsha/Porscha/Porsche: (Latin): offering
Posy: (English): God will increase
Precious: (American): treasured
Presley: (English): priest's land
Prima: (Latin): first, beginning
Primrose: (English): the first rose, primrose flower

Princess: (English): born to royalty
Priscilla: (Latin): from an ancient family
Prudence: (English): prudent or cautious
Pua: (Hawaiian): flower
Pyria: (American): cherished
Pythia: (Greek): prophet

Qi: (Chinese): fine jade
Qiana/Quiana: (American): living with grace, heavenly
Qiang: (Chinese): beautiful rose
Qing: (Chinese): dark blue
Quana: (Native American): sweet
Quarralia: (Australian): star
Quartilla: (Latin): fourth
Queen/Queenie/Quenna: (English): queen
Querida: (Spanish): dearly loved
Queta: (Spanish): head of the household
Quilla: (Incan): goddess of the moon
Quincy: (English): fifth-born child; (French): estate belonging to Quintus
Quinn: (Celtic): queenly; (Gaelic): one who provides counsel
Quintana/Quinella: (Latin): the fifth girl; (English): the queen's lawn
Quintessa: (Latin): of the essence

Rachel: (Hebrew): ewe; (Israel): innocent lamb
Racine: (French): root
Rae: (Scottish): grace; (German): wise protection
Raeden: (Japanese): thunder and lightning
Raelene/Rayleen: (American): a combination of Rae and Lee
Raelynn: (American): a form of Raylene
Rafaela/Raphaela: (Hebrew): healed by God
Rafiki: (African): friend
Rain/Raine/Raina: (American): blessings from above; (French & Latin): ruler; (English): lord, wise
Rainbow: (English): rainbow
Raisa: (Russian): a form of Rose
Raja: (Arabic): filled with hope
Ramona: (Spanish): wise protector
Randi: (English): shielded by wolves
Rani: (Sanskrit): queen
Ranita: (Hebrew): song, joyful
Raquel: (Spanish): innocent lamb
Rasha: (Arabic): resembling a young gazelle
Rashida: (Swahili & Turkish): righteous
Raven: (English): to be black, blackbird
Rayna: (Hebrew): pure; (Scandinavian): wise counsel
Razi: (Aramaic): secretive
Reagan: (Celtic): regal; (Irish): son of the small ruler
Reba: (Hebrew): fourth
Rebecca: (Biblical): servant of God
Rebel: (American): outlaw
Reese/Reece: (English & Welsh): ardent, fiery, enthusiastic
Regina: (Italian, Spanish & Latin America): queen
Rein: (German); advisor, counselor
Reina: (French & Spanish): queen; (English): wise ruler
Remi/Remy: (French): oarsman or rower from Rheims
Rena: (Hebrew): song
Renata: (French): a form of Renee, which means reborn

Renee: (French): reborn
Reta: (African): shaken
Reva: (Hebrew): rain
Reya: (Spanish): queenly
Reza: (Hungarian): harvester
Rhea: (Greek): rivers
Rhianna: (English): goddess; (Welsh): nymph
Rhiannon: (Welsh): pure maiden
Rhoda: (Greek): roses
Rhonda: (Welsh): carrying a good spear
Rhonwyn: (Irish): a form of Bronwyn, which means light-skinned
Ria: (Spanish): from the river's mouth
Richelle: (French): feminine form of Richard, which means strong ruler
Ricki/Rickelle: (American): a form of Erica, which means honorable ruler
Rielle: (Hebrew): a feminine form of Gabriel, which means God is my strength
Riley: (English): from the rye clearing; (Irish): a small stream
Rio: (Spanish & Portuguese): river
Rippina: (Japanese): brilliant light
Risa: (Latin): one who laughs often
Rita: (Greek): precious pearl
Riva: (French): river bank
River: (Latin & French): stream, water
Roberta: (English): bright with fame
Robin/Robyn: (English): a small bird
Rochelle: (French): from the little rock
Roja: (Spanish): red-haired woman
Rolanda: (German): well-known
Romina: (Arabian): from the Christian land
Romy: (French): a form of Rosemary, which means bitter rose
Rona: (Hebrew): my joy
Rong: (Chinese): martial
Rory: (Irish): famous brilliance, famous ruler; (Gaelic): red-haired
Rosa: (Spanish): rose
Rosalind/Rosalee: (Spanish): beautiful one
Rosario: (Filipino & Spanish): rosary
Rose: (English, French & Scottish): flower, a rose; (German): horse, fame
Roseanne/Rosanna: (Greek): graceful rose
Rosemary: (English): bitter rose
Rosetta: (Italian): rose
Roshonda/Roshawna: (American): a combination of Rose & Shawna
Rosina/Rosita: (Celtic): little rose
Roslyn/Rossalyn: (Scottish): cape, promontory
Rowan: (Irish): red-haired; (English & Gaelic): from the rowan tree
Rowena: (Welsh): fair and slender: (German): happy and famous
Roxanne: (Persian): sunrise
Roz/Roza: (Polish): rose
Ruby: (English & French): a precious jewel, a ruby
Rue: (Greek): herb of grace
Rula: (Latin & English): ruler
Rumer: (English); gypsy
Ruth: (Hebrew & Israel): companion, friend
Rylan: (English): the place where rye is grown
Rylee/Rylie: (Irish): a form of Riley, which means a small stream

Sabine/Sabina: (Latin): a tribe in ancient Italy
Sable: (English): sleek

Sabrina: (English): legendary princess
Sada: (Japanese): pure
Sadie: (English): a lady
Saffron: (English): resembling the yellow flower
Sahara: (Arabian): wilderness
Saige/Sage: (English & French): wise one; (English): from the spice
Sailor: (American): sailor
Sakari: (Native American & Hindi): sweet girl
Salina: (French): solemn, dignified
Sally/Sallie: (English): princess
Saloma/Salome: (Hebrew): peace and tranquility
Samantha: (Hebrew & Biblical): listener of God
Samina: (Hindi): happiness
Samira: (Arabic): entertaining
Sandra: (Greek): helper of humanity; (English): unheeded prophetess
Sandrine: (Greek): defender of mankind
Saniya: (Indian): a moment in time preserved
Santana: (Spanish): saintly
Santina: (Spanish): little saint
Sapphira/Sapphire: (Hebrew): sapphire; (Israel): beautiful
Sara(h): (Hebrew, Spanish & Biblical): princess
Sarafina/Saraphina: (Greek): gentle wind
Sardinia: (Italian): from the mountainous island
Sasha: (English): defender of mankind
Sato: (Japanese): sugar
Savannah: (Spanish): open plain, field
Sayo: (Japanese): born at night
Scarlett: (English): red
Scout: (French): scout
Season: (Latin): a fertile woman
Sedona: (American): the American city
Sela(h): (Israel): pause and reflect
Selene/Selena/Seline/Selina: (Greek): of the moon
Selma: (Scandinavian): divinely protected
Sena: (Persian): blessed
Sequoia: (Cherokee): giant redwood tree
Seraphina: (Israel): burning fire; (Hebrew): fiery-ringed
Serefina: (Latin): a winged angel
Serena/Syrena/Sirena: (Latin): peaceful disposition; (African American): calm, tranquil
Serenity: (Latin & English): peaceful
Shaba: (Spanish): rose
Shada: (Native American): pelican
Shae/Shea/Shay/Shayla: (Celtic & Irish): gift
Shahina: (Arabic): falcon
Shaina: (Yiddish): beautiful
Shakila: (Arabic): beautiful one
Shakira: (Arabic): grateful
Shamara: (Arabic): ready for battle
Shana/Shanea/Shanae: (Hebrew): God is gracious
Shandy/Shandie/Shandi: (English): rambunctious
Shane: (Hebrew): gift from God; (Irish): God is gracious
Shanel/Shanell/Shanelle/Shannel: (American): a form of Chanel, which means from the canal
Shani: (African): marvelous
Shania: (Native American): on my way
Shanika: (American): a combination of Sha and Nika

Shannon/Shannen: (Gaelic): having ancient wisdom
Sharlene: (English & French): manly, from the name Charles
Sharon: (Hebrew & Israel): a flat clearing
Shasta: (Native American): from the triple-peaked mountain
Shawn: (Irish): a form of Sean, which means God is gracious
Shawnee: (Native American): name of tribe
Shawnda: (English): God is gracious
Shaylee: (Gaelic): fairy princess
Sheba: (Hebrew): an ancient country in Arabia
Sheena: (Gaelic): God's gracious gift
Sheila/Sheela: (English & Irish): blind; (Italian): music
Shelby: (English): from the willow farm
Shelley/Shelly/Shellie: (English): meadow on the ledge
Sheridan: (Irish, English & Celtic): untamed; (Gaelic): bright, a seeker
Sherry/Sheree/Sheri/Sherri: (Israel): beloved; (French): dear one
Sheryl/Cheryl: (English): beloved
Shiloh: (Hebrew): he who was sent, God's gift, the one to whom it belongs; (Israel): peaceful
Shilpa: (Indian): well proportioned
Shima: (Japanese): true intention
Shirley: (English): bright meadow
Shona/Shonda: (Irish): a form of Jane, which means gift from God
Shoshana: (Arabic): white lily
Shu: (Chinese): kind, gentle
Shula: (Arabic): flaming, bright
Shura: (Russian): defender of mankind
Sibley: (English): sibling, friendly
Sibyl/Sybil/Cybil: (English): a seer or prophetess
Sidney/Sydney: (French): from Saint Denis
Sienna: (Italian): reddish brown in color
Sierra: (Spanish): mountain; (Irish): dark
Signe/Signy: (Latin): sign
Signourney: (English): victorious conquerer
Silvia/Sylvia: (Latin): forest
Silver: (English): precious metal
Simone: (French): one who listens well
Sinead: (Irish): gift from God
Siobhan: (Irish): gift from God
Siri: (Scandinavian): beautiful victory
Skye: (English): sky
Skylar/Skyler: (English): a scholar
Sloan: (English): raid; (Irish, Celtic, Scottish & Gaelic): fighter, warrior
Snow: (American): frozen rain
Solana: (Latin): from the east; (Spanish): sunshine
Solange: (French): religious and dignified
Soledad: (Spanish): solitary
Solita: (Latin): solitary
Sondra: (Greek): defender of mankind
Song: (Chinese): pine tree
Sonja/Sonia/Sonya: (Scandinavian): wisdom
Sonora: (Spanish): pleasant sounding
Sophia/Sofia/Sophie: (Greek & Biblical): wisdom
Sophie: (Greek): wisdom
Sora: (Native American): chirping songbird
Sorina: (Romanian): sun
Spencer/Spenser: (English): dispenser of provisions
Spica: (Latin): ear of wheat, a star in the constellation Virgo

Spring: (English): the spring season
Stacy/Stacey: (English): productive, resurrection
Starr: (English & American): star
Stella: (French, Italian & Greek): star
Stephanie: (Greek): crowned in victory
Stevie: (English & American): from the name Steven, which means crowned one
Stormy: (English): tempest; (American): impetuous nature
Suki: (Japanese): loved one
Sula: (Icelandic): large sea bird
Summer: (English): the summer season
Suni: (Zuni): native, a member of our tribe
Sunshine: (English): brilliant rays from the sun
Suri: (Todas): pointy nose
Surya: (Sanskrit): a sun god
Susan/Suzanne/Susannah/Suzie: (Hebrew): graceful lily; (Israel): lily
Sybil: (Greek): prophet
Sydney: (English): wide island
Sylvia/Silvia: (Latin): forest
Tabitha/Tabatha/Tabbitha: (Hebrew): beauty, grace; (Israel): a gazelle
Tacita/Taci/Tacey: (Latin): silent
Taffline/Taffy: (Welsh): beloved
Tahira: (Arabic): virginal, pure
Tai: (Chinese): large; (Vietnamese): prosperous, talented
Taima: (Native American): clash of thunder
Taja/Tajah: (Hindi): crowned
Taka: (Japanese): borrowed
Takenya: (Hebrew): animal horn
Taki: (Japanese): waterfall
Takia: (Arabic): worshipper
Tala: (Native American): a stalking wolf
Talia/Tahlia: (Hebrew): morning dew from heaven; (Greek): blooming
Talisa/Talissa: (American): consecrated to God
Talisha: (American): damsel, innocent
Tallis: (French & English): forest
Tallulah: (Choctaw): leaping water
Tama: (Japanese): precious stone
Tamaka: (Japanese): bracelet
Tamara/Tamra/Tamyra/Tammy: (Hebrew): palm tree; (Israel): spice
Tameka: (Aramaic): twin
Tamika/Tamiko: (Japanese): child of the people
Tamira: (Hebrew): palm tree, spice
Tandy: (English): team
Tangia: (American): angel
Tani: (Japanese): valley
Tania/Tonya/Tanya: (Slovakian): a fairy queen
Tanisha: (English): worthy of praise
Tao: (Chinese & Vietnamese): peach
Tara/Tari/Tarin/Tarryn: (Irish & Scottish): a hill where the kings meet
Tasha: (Greek): born on Christmas day
Tatiana: (Slavic): fairy queen
Tatum: (English): joyful, spirited
Taura: (Latin): bull
Tavi: (Aramaic): well-behaved
Tawny/Tawnee: (Gypsy): little one: (English): brownish yellow, tan
Tayanita: (Cherokee): beaver

Taylor: (English & French): a tailor
Teagan: (Gaelic): handsome, attractive
Temperance: (English): temperate, moderate
Tempest/Tempestt: (French): stormy
Terelle: (German): thunder ruler
Teresa/Theresa: (Finnish): summer, harvester; (Greek): reaper
Terrene: (Latin): smooth
Terrwyn: (Welsh): valiant
Tertia: (Latin): third
Tess/Tessa: (English): harvester
Thalia: (Greek): plentiful, blooming
Thea: (Greek): gift of God
Thelma: (English): ambitious, nurturing
Thema: (African): queen
Theodora: (English): gift of God
Theora: (Greek): a watcher
Theta: (Greek): eighth letter of the alphabet
Thomasina: (Hebrew): a twin
Thora: (Scandinavian): thunder
Tia: (Greek); princess; (Spanish): princess, aunt; (African American): aunt
Tiana: (Greek): princess
Tiara: (Latin): crowned
Tiegen: (Aztec) : princess
Tierney: (Gaelic): regal, lordly
Tiffany: (Greek): lasting love
Tijuana: (Spanish): border town in Mexico
Tilda: (English): strength in battle
Timothea: (English): honoring God
Tina: (English): river
Ting: (Chinese): graceful and slim
Tipper: (Irish): water pourer
Tira: (Hindi): arrow
Tirranna: (Australian): stream of water
Tirza: (Hebrew): pleasant
Tisa: (Swahili): ninth-born
Tisha/Tish: (Latin): joy
Tobi/Toby: (Hebrew): God is good
Toki: (Japanese & Korean): one who grabs opportunity
Tola: (Polish): praiseworthy
Tomiko: (Japanese): wealthy
Tomo: (Japanese): intelligent
Tomoko: (Japanese): two friends
Toni: (Greek): flourishing; (Latin): praise-worthy
Tonia/Tonya: (Slavic): fairy queen
Topagna: (Native American): from above
Topaz/Topaza: (Mexican): golden gem
Tory/Tori: (American): victorious
Toshi: (Japanese): mirror image
Tova/Tovah: (Hebrew): well-behaved
Tracy/Tracey: (English): brave
Trang: (Vietnamese): intelligent
Treasa: (Irish): great strength
Trevina: (Irish): prudent; (Welsh): homestead
Trina: (Greek): pure
Trinity: (Latin): the holy three
Trish/Trisha: (English & Latin): noble

Trixie: (American): a form of Beatrice, which means blessed
Trudy: (German): adored warrior
Tryna: (Greek): third-born child
Tula: (Hindi): balance
Tully: (Irish): at peace with God
Twila/Twyla: (English): woven of double thread
Tyne: (English): of the river Tyne
Tyra: (Scandinavian): God of battle; (Scottish): land

Ualani: (Hawaiian): rain from heaven
Udele: (English): prosperous
Ugolina: (German): bright mind and spirit
Ula: (Irish): sea jewel
Ulima: (Arabic): wise, astute
Ulrica: (German): wolf ruler
Ultima: (Latin): last
Ulva: (German): wolf
Uma: (Hindi): mother
Umiko: (Japanese): child of the sea
Una: (Welsh & Celtic): white wave; (Irish): unity: (Native American): remember; (English): one
Unique/Unika/Uniqua: (Latin): only one; (American): unlike others
Unity: (American): unity, togetherness
Urbana: (Latin): from the city
Uriana: (Greek): heaven, the unknown
Uriel: (Hebrew): light of God
Urika: (Omaha): useful
Ursula: (Danish & Scandinavian): female bear
Uta: (German): rich; (Japanese): poem
Utina: (Native American): woman of my country
Uzzia: (Hebrew): God is my strength

Vail: (English): valley
Vala: (German): chosen one
Valencia/Valentina/Valene: (Spanish & Italian): brave; (Latin America): health or love
Valeria/Valerie/Valery: (French): brave, fierce one; (English): strong, valiant
Vanessa: (Greek): resembling a butterfly
Vanity: (English): excessive pride
Vanna (Cambodian): golden
Vanora: (Welsh): white wave:
Vara: (Scandinavian): careful
Veda: (Sanskrit): sacred lore
Vega: (Arabic): falling star
Venecia/Venetia: (Italian): from Venice
Venus: (Greek): love goddess, little bird
Vera: (Russian): verity, truth
Verda: (Latin): young and fresh
Verna: (English): alder tree
Verena/Verity: (Latin): truthful
Veronica: (Latin): displaying a true image
Vespera: (Latin): evening star
Vesta: (Latin): keeper of the house
Victoria/Vicki/Vicky/Vickie: (Latin America): winner
Victory: (Latin): victory
Vienna: (Latin America): from wine country
Vignette: (French): from the little vine
Villette: (French): small town

Vina: (Hindi): musical instrument; (Spanish): vineyard
Viola: (Italian): violet flower
Violet: (French): resembling the flower
Violeta: (Bulgarian): violet
Virgilia: (Latin): staff bearer
Virginia: (English, Spanish, Italian & Latin America): pure
Vita: (Latin): life
Viv: (Latin America): alive
Viveka/Viveca: (German): little woman of the strong fortress
Vivian: (Latin): lively
Vivianne/Vivienne/Vivian/Vivien: (English): the lady of the lake
Vixen: (American): flirtatious
Vonna: (French): young archer; (Latin): true image

Wallis: (English): from Wales
Wanda: (German): wanderer
Waneta: (Native American): charger
Wanetta: (English): pale face
Waynette: (English): wagon maker
Wednesday: (American): born on a Wednesday
Wen: (Chinese): refinement
Wendy: (English): white-skinned, literary
Wesley: (English): western meadow
Whisper: (English): soft-spoken
Whitley: (English): from the white meadow
Whitney: (English & African American): white island
Wilhelmina/Wilma: (German): resolute protector
Willa: (English): protector
Willow: (English): willow tree
Winetta: (American): peaceful
Wing: (Chinese): glory
Winifred: (Irish): friend of peace; (Welsh): reconciled, blessed
Winnie: (Irish & Celtic): white, fair
Winola: (German): gracious and charming
Wren: (Welsh): ruler; (English): small bird
Wynonna/Winona: (American): oldest daughter

Xanadu: (African): from the exotic paradise
Xantara: (American): protector of the earth
Xanthe: (Greek): yellow, blond
Xaviera: (Arabic): bright
Xema: (Latin): precious
Xena/Xenia: (Greek): hospitable
Xenosa: (Greek): stranger
Xerena: (Latin): peaceful disposition
Xiang: (Chinese): pleasant fragrance
Ximena: (Greek): heroine
Xiu: (Chinese): grace
Xoana: (Hebrew): God is compassionate and merciful
Xuan: (Vietnamese): spring
Xyleena: (Greek): forest dweller

Yadira: (Hebrew): friend
Yadra: (Spanish): mother
Yael: (Hebrew): strength of God
Yaffa: (Hebrew): beautiful

Yalena: (Greek): shining light
Yama: (Japanese): from the mountain
Yaminta: (Native American): minty
Yamka: (Hopi): blossom
Yamuna: (Hindi): sacred river
Yana: (Hebrew): he answers
Yanaba: (Navajo): brave
Yang: (Chinese): sun
Yanessa: (American): resembling a butterfly
Yara: (Brazilian): goddess of the river; (Iranian): courage
Yashira: (Japanese): blessed with God's grace; (Afghan): humble
Yasmine/Yasmeen: (Persian): resembling the jasmine flower
Yei: (Japanese): flourishing
Yeira: (Hebrew): light
Yelena: (Russian): a form of Helen, which means light
Yen: (Chinese): yearning
Yenay: (Chinese): she who loves
Yeo: (Korean): mild
Yepa: (Native American): snow girl
Yesenia: (Arabic): flower
Yessica: (Hebrew): the Lord sees all
Yetta: (English): ruler of the house
Yin: (Chinese): silver
Yitta: (Hebrew): one who emanates light
Yoki: (Native American): of the rain, bluebird
Yoko: (Japanese): good girl
Yolanda: (Greek): resembling the violet flower
Yon: (Korean): lotus blossom
Yori: (Japanese): reliable
Yoshi: (Japanese): respectful and good
Yu: (Chinese): universe
Yuki: (Japanese): snow
Yukiko: (Japanese): happy child
Yumiko: (Japanese): beautiful and helpful child
Yuna: (African): gorgeous
Yuri: (Japanese): lily
Yvette/Ivette: (French): a form of Yvonne, which means young archer
Yvonne: (French): young archer

Zaba: (Hebrew): she who offers a sacrifice to God
Zada: (Arabic): prosperous
Zahara: (Arabic): shining, luminous, the bright dawn
Zaidee: (Arabic): rich
Zakia: (Swahili): smart; (Arabic): chaste
Zakila: (Swahili): born to royalty
Zakiyyah: (Muslim): sharp, intellectual, pious, pure
Zaltana: (Native American): high mountain
Zana: (Romanian): the three graces
Zara: (Hebrew & Israel): princess
Zaynah: (Arabic): beautiful
Zelda: (Yiddish): gray-haired
Zelene: (Greek): sunshine
Zelia: (Greek): having zeal; (Spanish): of the sunshine
Zelmira: (Arabic): brilliant
Zemira: (Hebrew & Israel): praised
Zena: (African): famous; (Greek): hospitable; (Persian): woman; (Ethiopian): news

Zenda: (Persian): sacred, feminine
Zenia: (Greek): hospitable
Zenobia: (Greek): child of Zeus
Zephrine: (English): breeze
Zephyr: (Greek): of the west wind
Zera: (Hebrew): seeds
Zerlina: (Latin & Spanish): beautiful dawn
Zesta: (American): with zest or gusto
Zeta: (English): rose
Zetta: (Portuguese): rose
Zi: (Chinese): flourishing, beautiful, with grace
Zia: (Arabic): one who emanates light
Zila: (Hebrew): shadow, shade
Zilla/Zillah: (Hebrew): shadows, shade
Zina: (African): secret spirit; (English): hospitable, welcoming
Zinnia: (English): the flower: (Latin America): beautiful
Zipporah: (Hebrew & Israel): bird
Zita: (Spanish): little rose
Ziva: (Hebrew): bright, radiant
Zoe/Zoey/Zooey: (Greek): life, alive
Zola: (Mexican): Earth; (French): famous bearer
Zora: (Slavic): sunrise
Zoya: (Greek): life
Zudora: (Sanskrit): laborer
Zula: (African): brilliant
Zuri: (French): lovely and white

www.ingramcontent.com/pod-product-compliance
Lightning Source LLC
LaVergne TN
LVHW081354060426
835510LV00013B/1822